AF413827

AUTHORITY BOOKS

How To Dominate Your Entire Industry With One Well-Crafted Book

AUTHORITY BOOKS

How To Dominate Your Entire Industry With One Well-Crafted Book

GIOVANNI PHILIPOSE

Jacket Design, Photography, Illustrations, and Interior Layout by Giovanni Philipose

ISBN: 979-8-9955278-0-0

DISCLAIMER:
The information provided in this book is for educational and informational purposes only. The author, publisher, and licensed distributor have made reasonable efforts to ensure that the information within was accurate at the time of publication. The author, publisher, and licensed distributor make no representation or warranties with respect to the merchantability, fitness for a particular purpose, current or continued accuracy or completeness, and reliability of the contents of this book.

The strategies, tips, and tools discussed in this book are the author's personal opinions and are provided as-is. They are intended to provide helpful and informative material on the subjects addressed in this book. Success in any marketing and business endeavors is based on a wide range of factors unique to each individual or business.

Laws are subject to change and may vary by location and jurisdiction. You, as the reader, are encouraged to consult with a professional where appropriate and review the current local laws before implementing any marketing strategies or campaigns.

Earnings and income representations made by the author are aspirational statements only of your potential earnings. The success of the author and others referenced herein, testimonials, and other examples used are exceptional, non-typical results and are not intended to be and are not a guarantee that you or others will achieve the same results. Individual results will always vary and your results will depend entirely on your individual capacity, work ethic, business, skills and experience, level of motivation, diligence in applying the strategies discussed, the economy, the normal and unforeseen risks of doing business, and other factors within or beyond your control.

damages, regardless of whether arising directly or indirectly from the use and/or misuse of this book. Readers agree to release and hold harmless the Company and its members, employees, agents, representatives, affiliates, subsidiaries, successors, and assignees (collectively "Agents") from and against any and all claims, liabilities, losses, causes of actions, costs, lost profits, lost opportunities, indirect, special, incidental, consequential, punitive, or any other damages whatsoever and expenses (including, without limitation, court costs and attorney's fees) ("Losses") asserted against, resulting from, imposed upon or incurred by any of the Agents as a result of, or arising out of the reader's use and/or misuse of this book. This book is intended for informational and educational purposes only.

HYPOTHETICAL PERFORMANCE RESULTS HAVE MANY INHERENT LIMITATIONS, SOME OF WHICH ARE DESCRIBED BELOW. NO REPRESENTATION IS BEING MADE THAT ANY BUSINESS WILL OR IS LIKELY TO ACHIEVE PROFITS OR LOSSES SIMILAR TO THOSE SHOWN OR DESCRIBED. IN FACT, THERE ARE FREQUENTLY SHARP DIFFERENCES BETWEEN HYPOTHETICAL PERFORMANCE RESULTS AND THE ACTUAL RESULTS SUBSEQUENTLY ACHIEVED BY ANY PARTICULAR BUSINESS. ONE OF THE LIMITATIONS OF HYPOTHETICAL PERFORMANCE RESULTS IS THAT THEY ARE GENERALLY PREPARED WITH THE BENEFIT OF HINDSIGHT. IN ADDITION, HYPOTHETICAL BUSINESS DOES NOT INVOLVE FINANCIAL RISK, AND NO HYPOTHETICAL BUSINESS RECORD CAN COMPLETELY ACCOUNT FOR THE IMPACT OF FINANCIAL RISK IN ACTUAL BUSINESS. FOR EXAMPLE, THE ABILITY TO WITHSTAND LOSSES OR TO ADHERE TO A PARTICULAR BUSINESS STRATEGY IN SPITE OF BUSINESS LOSSES ARE MATERIAL POINTS WHICH CAN ALSO ADVERSELY AFFECT ACTUAL BUSINESS RESULTS. THERE ARE NUMEROUS OTHER FACTORS RELATED TO THE MARKETS IN GENERAL OR TO THE IMPLEMENTATION OF ANY SPECIFIC BUSINESS PROGRAM, WHICH CANNOT BE FULLY ACCOUNTED FOR IN THE PREPARATION OF HYPOTHETICAL PERFORMANCE. When used herein, this "book" means this book, its contents, and all information and ideas contained therein.

There are authors.
Then there are **_authors with author-ity_**.
We help entrepreneurs, business owners, and experts become the latter.
Want to launch your Authority Book?

Follow the road ahead...and good luck!

DEDICATION

For God, I hope to lead by example and make you proud.

For Elizabeth, your relentless work ethic, unconditional love, and pure selflessness inspire me on the daily. I respect everything you stand for and am eternally grateful I get to spend the rest of my life around someone of your caliber. I love you always. Cheers to the future, let's work.

For Rafa, my 90-lb German Shepherd puppy and best friend. Thanks for keeping me grounded as I worked on this project. I'll give you a treat here in a minute. Love you bud.

CONTENTS

AUTHORITY BOOKS

How To Dominate Your Entire Industry With One Well-Crafted Book

GIOVANNI PHILIPOSE

START HERE

I wrote and published this book when I was 21 years old.

I wrote and published THIS book when I was 22 years old.

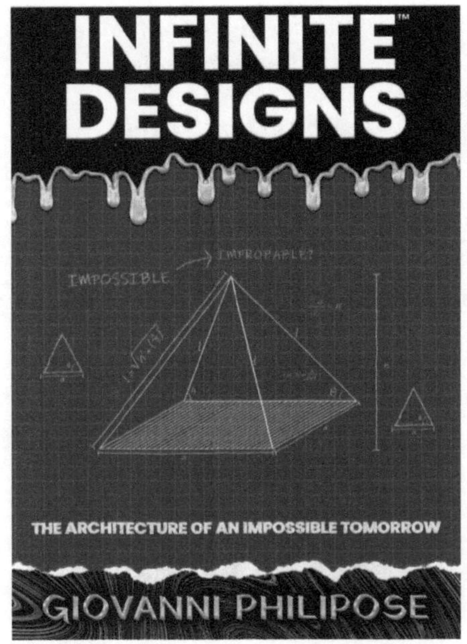

Fast forward to today, at the time of writing this book…

…I am 23 years old.

Although I have many more books to write…and much more to learn…I would like to, with your permission, share one tiny thing I've learned throughout this process:

Words, if articulated and interwoven correctly, can move *the mountains, masses, minds, and missions of the world.*

But in business, money talks. Sometimes, louder than words…

So I'll amend my original statement to this: Words, if articulated and interwoven correctly, can move the mountains, masses, minds, missions…*and markets*…of the world.

SAID DIFFERENTLY:

If you can move the masses, you can move the markets.

And if you can move markets, you can move money.

To be clear, it's not about manipulation. *It's about communication*.

Most of history's greatest leaders, entrepreneurs, and icons were powerful communicators. In fact, their ability *to communicate* is likely what made them great leaders, entrepreneurs, and icons in the first place. However, some of history's greatest dictators, conquerors, emperors, criminals, and more…*were also powerful communicators.* As the quote above this brief chapter mentions, words have been, are, and always will be the source of both beautiful and catastrophic consequences. And round and round the world turns…

Haven't you ever heard a speech that moved your soul?
Haven't you ever read a book that transformed your mind?
Haven't you ever watched a movie that changed your life?
Haven't you ever heard a song that revitalized your very sense of being?

See…

- → **Cinema**
- → **Speeches**

→ **Poems**
→ **Music**
→ **Theatre**
→ **Books**
→ **Etc.**

...are but a few examples of how words, if articulated and interwoven correctly, can move the world...*for better or for worse.*

With regard to business and entrepreneurship...

→ **Marketing**
→ **Branding**
→ **Client Acquisition**

...all fundamentally rely on one's ability to articulate and interweave words together effectively, efficiently, and above all else...ethically.

The rewards for doing so are impossible to count. So, to keep it brief, I'll limit it to **The Three I's**...

1. **Impact** - *Describes what you do for others.*
2. **Income** - *Describes what is given in exchange for goods and services.*
3. **Identity** - *Describes who you become in the process.*

That's the beautiful game of entrepreneurship. Serve others, make money while doing so, and become a better person throughout the process.

With an **Authority Book**, you can play the game...at scale. Bigger, better, badder, and everything in between. That's my offer.

This book is subtitled *"How To Dominate Your Entire Industry With One Well-Crafted Book."* Whether you're an entrepreneur, business owner, investor, expert...or all of the above...the contents laid throughout the following pages are designed to follow through on the aforementioned promise. You can count on that.

This book is my **Authority Book.** Study closely, and let the magic begin.

THE ROADMAP

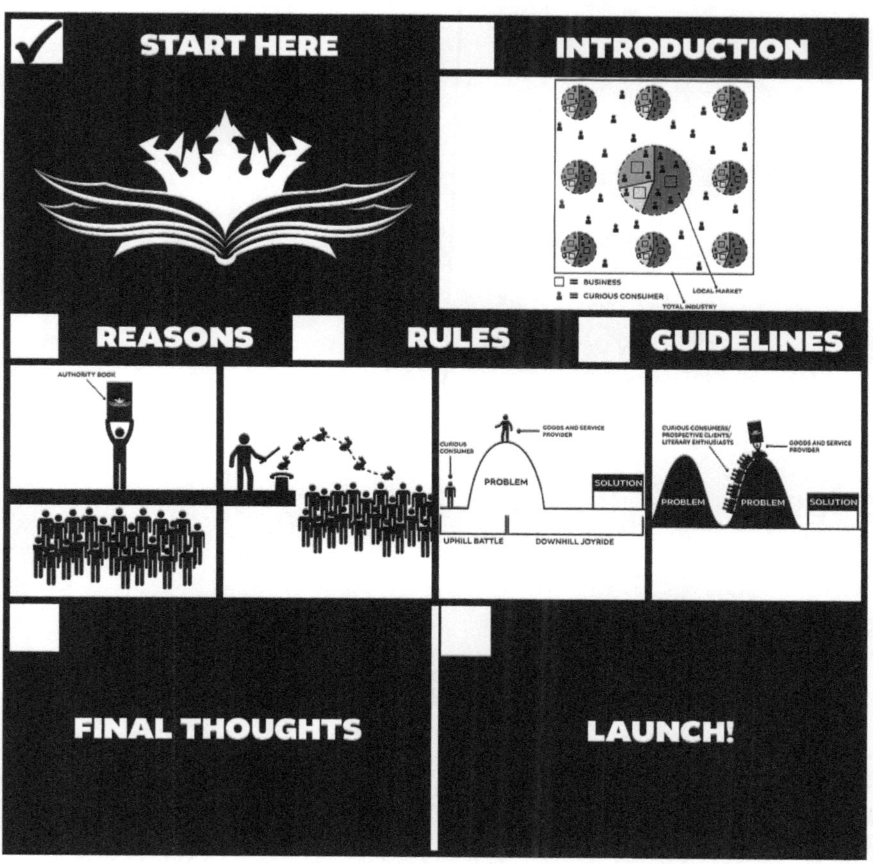

START HERE
INTRODUCTION
BUSINESS
CURIOUS CONSUMER
LOCAL MARKET
TOTAL INDUSTRY
REASONS
RULES
GUIDELINES
AUTHORITY BOOK
CURIOUS CONSUMER
GOODS AND SERVICE PROVIDER
PROBLEM
SOLUTION
UPHILL BATTLE
DOWNHILL JOYRIDE
CURIOUS CONSUMERS/ PROSPECTIVE CLIENTS/ LITERARY ENTHUSIASTS
GOODS AND SERVICE PROVIDER
PROBLEM
PROBLEM
SOLUTION
FINAL THOUGHTS
LAUNCH!

SECTION I:

INTRODUCTION

5 YEARS IN 5 PAGES

> *"Rock bottom became the solid foundation on which I rebuilt my life."*
>
> *— J.K. Rowling —*

"Fail forward" summarizes my personal philosophy over the last 5 years quite well. I carried a delusional conviction that if I could embrace failure and endure the public shame/humiliation/passive-aggressive comments that came with pursuing a non-traditional path long enough to master my craft, then I could bring my visions to life. Suffering builds character. *At least, that's what I told myself...*

My passion for *tactical performance-based psychology, timeless wisdom, and accessible education* was the driving force for launching GPA Enterprises (GPAENTERPRISES.COM).

My passion for...

- → **The Battle for Market Share (AKA marketing/branding/client acquisition)**
- → **The Magical Art of Writing, Printing, and Publishing**

...and playing the game of entrepreneurship *at scale* was the driving force for launching Authority Book Launch (AUTHORITYBOOKLAUNCH.COM).

To give you more context...

HOW WE GOT HERE

MARCH 4, 2026 - 6 A.M.

As I woke up on my 23rd birthday, I noticed nothing felt different. A year had passed, yet I felt...*the same*. To help you better understand the gravity of this statement, let me recap the last few years of my life in less than 60 seconds...

AGE 18

→ As an ambitious yet lost kid in high school, I worked relentlessly for a delusional future. I was an all-state soccer player and valedictorian. I scored a 35 on the ACT and became an Oklahoma State Regents Scholar, which, in dollars, was roughly worth over $55,000.

Yet, I was still lost...

→ Nevertheless, the scholarship led me to the University of Oklahoma, where I met Elizabeth—my ride-or-die, soulmate, and now lovely fiancée—who you'll hear me rave about for as long as I walk this Earth.

AGE 20-21

→ Moved into my own apartment with Elizabeth in Downtown OKC
→ Graduated Summa Cum Laude with a 4.0 from the University of Oklahoma in three years after completing the pre-med curriculum with a B.A. in Psychology

Yet, I still felt this insatiable hunger to learn...

→ Decided to set out to learn and acquire any/all skills required to launch my own business instead of going to medical school to become a psychiatrist
→ Launched GPA Enterprises, my media & publishing company, before I possessed the skills required to bring my visions to life

And here's where it gets fun...

JULY 2024 - DECEMBER 2024

Started to learn and acquire said skills such as...

- → Website design
- → Organic marketing
- → Branding
- → Client acquisition
- → Video editing & production
- → Graphic design
- → And most importantly...**The Magical Art of Writing, Printing, and Publishing** (which we'll cover in greater detail in a few chapters)

Essentially, the ABCs and 123s of business, organic marketing, and publishing...

"Fail Forward"..."Fail Forward"..."Fail Forward"...

JANUARY 2025

- → Wrote and published a 50-page manuscript on Amazon with my head held high...for now. Proud to be a 21-year-old Author...but is 50 pages really a book? So I went back to the lab to improve... because the truth was, I wasn't good enough. Not by my standards. *Not by a long shot.*

JANUARY 2025 - JANUARY 2026

- → 12 months of skill acquisition and refining my craft. I learned how to print and publish quality books with *a cloth hardcover, thick cream paper, and a 1000x better book cover*...all for the 184-page manuscript of my first real book: **INFINITE DESIGNS.**
- → Also adopted my now 90-lb German Shepherd, Rafael (we call him Rafa, but *"The Beast"* from *The Sandlot* works too).

But here's where it gets rocky...

FEBRUARY 2026

- First, a snowstorm delayed print centers for an **ENTIRE MONTH**.
- Then, I received a rejection email for a Ph.D. graduate program in Clinical Psychology.
- Not too long after, I received **ANOTHER** rejection email for a Psy.D. graduate program in Clinical Psychology.

Not my finest month, as you can presumably imagine.

Which leads us back to the beginning...

MARCH 5TH, 2026

The day after my birthday, I received the proof copy for my book (1 month later than expected) and...I've never felt prouder about anything in my entire life.

2 years of refining my craft, consolidating the wisdom of others into tactical skills, and failing forward... finally paid off!

The feeling was surreal. And this time, this book wasn't just going on Amazon. I learned how to get it into the online storefronts of the following stores: Walmart, Books-A-Million, Bookshop.org, and...Barnes & Freakin' Noble.

I mean, come on! Once again, it felt surreal, to say the least.

And that's when it clicked...

I knew what this was going to mean for my own media & publishing company...

- → **Impact** - *Describes what you do for others.*
- → **Income** - *Describes what is given in exchange for goods and services.*
- → **Identity** - *Describes who you become in the process.*

…but what if I took all the skills I learned…mistakes I made…wisdom I gained…

…WAIT, the rejection was just redirection!

What if I helped other entrepreneurs, business owners, and experts launch their OWN organic marketing asset?!

As I said before, it clicked:

→ **Every serious entrepreneur needs an Authority Book.**

So I grabbed my computer, jotted down my vision, built the corresponding infrastructure & systems…

…and AUTHORITYBOOKLAUNCH.COM was born.

AUTHORITY BOOKS 101

There are authors.
Then there are authors with author-ity. (get the joke?)

Allow me to humbly explain the difference…

In this chapter, we'll cover six things:

1. The Tragedy of The Author
2. The Problem(s) This Book Solves
3. The Battle for Market Share
4. The Problem(s) Your Authority Book Will Solve
5. My Hidden Agenda
6. The Roadmap

Without further delay, let's begin.

THE TRAGEDY OF THE AUTHOR

Question #1: How many books are published each year?

→ **Answer: Millions**

Question #2: How many copies of each book are sold on average?

→ **Answer: Hundreds**

Question #3: How many authors are failing?

→ **Answer: More than there are succeeding.**

Nonetheless, some books *do sell.* The "well-crafted" ones at least. And I'm not talking about the number of print copies, e-books, or even audiobooks sold.

I'm talking about branding. Books can sell consumers on you, your business, and your industry.

→ **Authority Books, if designed correctly, can sell goods, products, and services.**
→ **Authority Books, if designed correctly, can build credibility, brand, and legacy.**
→ **Authority Books, if designed correctly, can be used to dominate an entire industry.**

Call it science. Call it art. Call it magic.

It works. And it's necessary in the 21st century.

If you want to be the best in your respective market, at least.

THE PROBLEM(S) THIS BOOK SOLVES

This book is, in its purest form, a conversation between two individuals (entrepreneurs, to be specific).

Entrepreneur A: Me, Myself, and I

Entrepreneur B: You, Yourself, and U (get the joke?)

By writing this book, I am solving one major problem: *conversations at scale.*

Entrepreneur A stays the same regardless of who holds the book. But Entrepreneur B can hand this book to Entrepreneur C, Entrepreneur C can hand this book to Entrepreneur D, and on and on the organic marketing train will go!

But even if one of the entrepreneurs listed above decided to hoard all of the wisdom laid throughout the pages of this book for themselves, thus breaking the cycle of goodwill and preventing future entrepreneurs from being able to feed their families, put clothes on their children's backs, and put a roof over their heads…

Entrepreneur A (otherwise known as Me, Myself, and I) can market this book myself, thus having tens, hundreds, if not thousands of entrepreneurs (AKA potential clients) having a 1-on-1 conversation with me— the goods and services provider.

As I said earlier, ***conversations at scale.***

Not to mention the immeasurable impact made on the readers and their families, the communities that these entrepreneurs serve, and the **IN-FINITE** (referencing my other book series) ripple effects created as a by-product of the aforementioned outcomes.

All that from **ONE. WELL-CRAFTED. BOOK.**

Could I be stretching the positive consequences? Maybe.

But maybe not…? After all, you're reading it.

Books transcend time and space. Therefore, they retain value. Therefore, if you don't have one for your business, you need one. As in you need it by yesterday. If that's impossible, then ASAP will do.

And if telling you isn't enough, I'll show you. As they say, an image is worth 1,000 words.

So let's test that theory…

THE BATTLE FOR MARKET SHARE

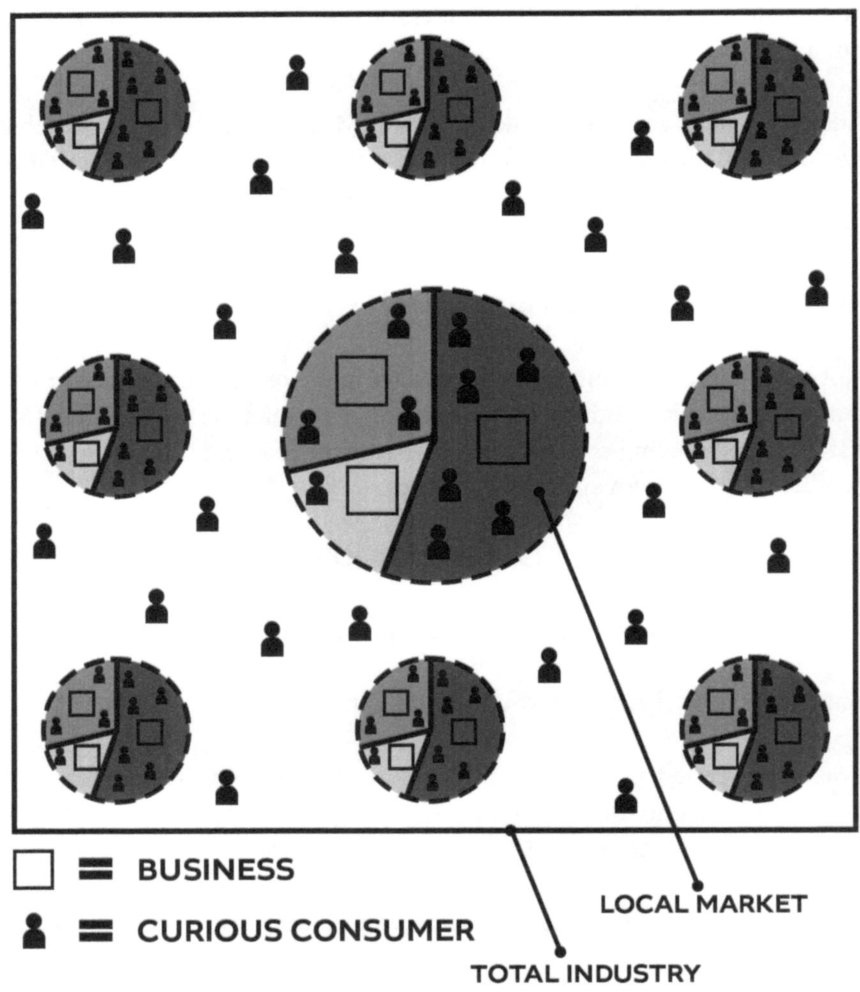

FIGURE 1: There are two key gladiator arenas with regard to marketing, branding, and client acquisition in every industry. The first is **The Battle for Local Market Share**. The second is **The Battle for Total Market Share**.

Many of you wake up in the morning with a singular objective:

MAKE MONEY

As entrepreneurs/business owners/investors, your role in the marketplace is to exchange goods and services for dollars…effectively, efficiently, and ethically.

Anything and everything that does not supplement or complement this objective, directly or indirectly, is, as the French would call it…a distraction. To clarify, it's pronounced "*dees-trak-syon*".

The world is full of them. They eat away at the mind, and steal your most precious asset…and no, I'm not talking about money. I'm talking about **attention**.

Now, as I said in the beginning, at the time of writing this book… I am 23 years old. Born in '03. So I have zero experience of the 20th Century.

Fortunately, we're in the 21st Century now. And let me tell you…it's all about **ATTENTION**. The marketplace does not necessarily belong to those who work the hardest or the longest. It belongs to those who know how to convert attention into dollars. Now, this statement might ring true to some of you…because it's been true long before I was born. It's commonly referred to as marketing.

But I have a better name for it…

The Battle for Market Share.

See, although popular technology changes throughout the decades, the fundamental principles of marketing remain the same.

The market belongs to the entrepreneurs/business owners/investors who know how to take it. Similar to the conquistadors and explorers of history, entrepreneurs **HAVE TO** seize territory in order to build/run/scale a business that can exchange goods and services for dollars.

The issue is that the game has changed.

Now, there are two forms of territory:

1. **Physical (Local Market)**
2. **Digital (Total Industry)**

Physical territory includes brick-and-mortar locations, billboards, seminars, flyers, events, etc. Essentially, anything that exists outside of a screen is, as we have defined, *physical* territory.

Digital territory, on the other hand, is summed up with a single letter:

I

Yes, I-Pads, I-Phones, and I-Pods but, to be clearer…anything that steals the focus from people's literal **EYE-BALLS.** Eyeballs are distributors of attention. And if you don't know how to get them to look at your business, you're screwed.

Fortunately, I have a solution.

It's called…**Authority Books.**

Authority Books allow you to have conversations at scale. But what exactly does this mean?

Question: How many entrepreneurs & business owners market on social media?

➔ **Answer: Millions**

Follow-up Question: How can you win the online battle for total market share?

➔ **Answer: By taking the conversation offline.**

As I said before, eyeballs are distributors of attention. And if you don't know how to get them to look at your business, you're screwed.

Online marketing is loud, chaotic, and distracting.
Offline marketing is quiet, calm, and focused.

Authority Books bridge online and offline marketing, branding, and client acquisition efforts.

Authority Books are powerful offline conversion tools for entrepreneurs and business owners to use when attempting to convert online eyeballs into clients.

Authority Books cut through the noise so you can deliver 1-on-1 value to an unlimited amount of potential clients *before* they become your actual clients.

Hence, why every serious entrepreneur needs one if they want to dominate their industry.

To be relatively straightforward, I don't care how you market your business.

Whether you…

- → **Run paid ads**
- → **Make business cards**
- → **Cold call**
- → **Print flyers**
- → **Deliver in-person proposals**
- → **Run brick-and-mortar locations**
- → **Speak at industry events**
- → **Host local events, giveaways, or other fun extravaganzas**
- → **Make social media content**
- → **Billboards**
- → **Start a podcast**
- → **SEO optimize your website**

…or do any of the other **INFINITE** (referring to my other book series) marketing, branding, and client acquisition related activities that cannot possibly be named in one sitting…you're still missing the most valuable asset of all.

You can do all that and more…but you still need an **Authority Book.**

If telling you isn't enough…I'll show you.

EXAMPLE 1:

Take Jimmy and Johnny.

Both are Certified Public Accountants (CPAs for short).

One runs a brick-and-mortar location in his local community.
The other does that too in the same community.

Here's the question: which one wins?

→ **Answer: Hard to tell.**

Some of you might want to look at their ad spend…or their alma mater…
or their website and logo…or a gazillion other things that may or may not
give you the right answer.

Simplify it.

Which one gets the most business?

→ **Answer: The one with more authority.**

To quantify authority, we can use…

THE AUTHORITY METRIC

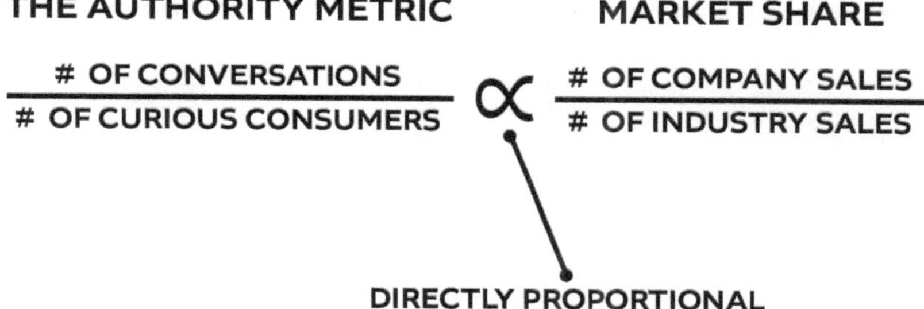

FIGURE 2: The goal, **when marketing**, is to convert eyeballs into conversations. The goal, **when selling**, is to convert conversations into dollars. **The Authority Metric** measures the bridge between the two processes, especially with regard to online marketing, due to both the volume of competition and the volume of curious consumers. Said differently, **The Authority Metric** is a strong predictor of future market share.

Let's expand on the aforementioned example…

Take Jimmy and Johnny.

Both are Certified Public Accountants (CPAs for short).

One runs a brick-and-mortar location in his local community.
The other does that too in the same community.

This last year, there were 100 prospective local clients looking for an accountant.

Johnny advertised, marketed, and acquired new clients *the old-fashioned way.*

He took a few of them out to dinner, met some others out for a couple of drinks, and eventually smooth-talked some of them into hiring him for the job.

You know…the works.

And Jimmy did the same. But he **ALSO** took 100 copies of his well-crafted **Authority Book** and gave them to each of the prospective clients…*for free.* Conversations at scale. Brilliant!

In the end, to be conservative in our example, let's say Jimmy won 60 of the new clients while Johnny won the remaining 40.

If we apply the commonly used formula, Jimmy stole an extra 10% of the local market share *by simply possessing* an **Authority Book**.

But what if it's not just Jimmy and Johnny competing for the same local community?

What if Jordan and Jessica want to feed their families, put clothes on their children's backs, and put a roof over their heads…

Individual market share will decrease…and decrease…and decrease…until the pie is asymmetrical.

At some point...whether it is a year or a decade...the market will look something like this:

→ **Jimmy single-handedly controls 50% of the market.**
→ **Meanwhile, Johnny, Jordan, and Jessica are all fighting over the leftovers.**

In this case, ***Jimmy has won the local battle for market share.***

Jimmy...for better or for worse...is the local authority of accounting.

THE PROBLEM(S) YOUR AUTHORITY BOOK WILL SOLVE

You may not need an **Authority Book** to win **The Battle for Local Market Share**. It would make things easier, absolutely. But it's not necessary. For many of you, you managed to do that yourself...the old-fashioned way. I have nothing but respect for entrepreneurs who built their business from the ground up with discipline, integrity, and a relentless work ethic.

But as we said earlier, ***there are two battles*** that are occurring at any given moment...

1. **The Battle for Local Market Share**
2. **The Battle for Total Market Share**

You don't need an **Authority Book** to dominate your local market.

However, you do need an **Authority Book** to dominate your entire industry.

To put this in perspective, let's enter **EXAMPLE 2:**

EXAMPLE 2:

Let's say Jimmy, Johnny, Jordan, and Jessica are invited to their state's "Annual Accounting Seminar," for lack of a better title.

And at this conference...are 996 ***other*** accountants.

Here's the question: What makes one different from the other?

→ **Answer: Hard to tell (from the client's POV)**

Some of you might want to look at their ad spend…or their alma mater… or their website and logo…or a gazillion other things that may or may not give you the right answer.

Simplify it.

Which one gets the most business?

→ **Answer: The one with more authority.**

Imagine 100 prospective clients walk into the conference looking for an accountant. And they have 1,000 options to choose from…quite literally.

But you are granted 30 seconds of stage time to battle the other 999 competitors for market share.

30 seconds to potentially win 100 clients. Do the math on the average LTV of a single client. Then multiply that by 100. ***That's what is at stake.***

So, how should you try to win the business?

→ **Not by talking about your business…others will do that.**
→ **Not by showboating your awards and trophies…others will do that.**

The answer is simple: you walk up and give a copy of your **Authority Book** to each client…**for FREE. Authority Books**…the world's greatest ice-breakers!

Think of it like a business card, resume, and proposal…all-in-one.

Once again, ***conversations at scale.***

Now take the previous example, and apply it to any/all online marketing, branding, and client acquisition efforts.

Can't you see the difference?

The easiest, and oftentimes only, way to separate yourself from your online competitors is to take the conversation offline, deliver value for 100-150 pages minimum, and let the rest take care of itself. Considering the readers are curious consumers who need to hire someone from your industry to solve their problem, the **Authority Book** merely bridges the online marketing efforts and the discovery call.

We'll speak on these ideas in greater detail later once we reach the tactical sections of this book.

For now, just remember: **Authority Books** bridge online and offline marketing, branding, and client acquisition efforts. Hence, why every serious entrepreneur needs one if they want to dominate their industry.

MY HIDDEN AGENDA

As I mentioned before, this book is my **Authority Book**. I figured, proof beats promise. This book in your hands is proof that what I offer...***works***. My objective is simple: to show you my hand...and still close the deal. No poker face...no hidden agenda...no funny business.

Just...un-funny business?

I guarantee that by the end of this book, if you are amongst the top 10% of your industry, you will want an **Authority Book** for your business.

And once the demand is created...I will supply a certain percentage of the entrepreneurs who read this book with any and all resources needed to help their dreams come true.

Marketing, branding, and client acquisition 101. Right in front of your eyes.

Call it science. Call it art. Call it magic.

It works. And if it works for my business, it'll probably work for yours too.

Consider this book my business card, my resume, my proposal, and my magic trick...***all-in-one***. As you read this book, study the details. Analyze the print quality. Step into my shoes. Imagine ***your*** words on paper in ***your*** prospective client's hands. Then multiply the number of prospective clients by 100. Then multiply that number by 100. And repeat this process until you understand the following sentence:

CONVERSATIONS. AT. SCALE.

That's what I offer. That's the power of one well-crafted book.

To conclude the introduction to this book, I'll end with this:

There are authors.
Then there are authors with author-ity.
We help entrepreneurs, business owners, and experts become the latter.

Want to launch your **Authority Book**?

Follow the road ahead…and good luck!

CHAPTER SUMMARY

- ☑ **Authority Books**, if designed correctly, can sell goods, products, and services.

- ☑ **Authority Books**, if designed correctly, can build credibility, brand, and legacy.

- ☑ **Authority Books**, if designed correctly, can be used to dominate an entire industry.

- ☑ Books transcend time and space. Therefore, they retain value. Therefore, if you don't have one for your business, you need one. As in you need it by yesterday. If that's impossible, then ASAP will do.

- ☑ There are two key gladiator arenas with regard to marketing,

- ☑ branding, and client acquisition in every industry. The first is **The Battle for Local Market Share**. The second is **The Battle for Total Market Share**.

- ☑ **Authority Books** allow you to have conversations at scale.

- ☑ **Authority Books** bridge online and offline marketing, branding, and client acquisition efforts.

- ☑ **Authority Books** are powerful offline conversion tools for entrepreneurs and business owners to use when attempting to convert online eyeballs into clients.

- ☑ **Authority Books** cut through the noise so you can deliver 1-on-1 value to an unlimited amount of potential clients before they become your actual clients.

- ☑ The goal, when marketing, is to convert eyeballs into conversations. The goal, when selling, is to convert conversations into dollars. **The Authority Metric** measures the bridge between the two processes, especially with regard to online marketing, due to both the volume of competition and the volume of curious consumers. Said differently, **The Authority Metric** is a strong predictor of future market share.

- ☑ You don't need an **Authority Book** to dominate your local market. However, you do need an **Authority Book** to dominate your entire industry.

THE ROADMAP

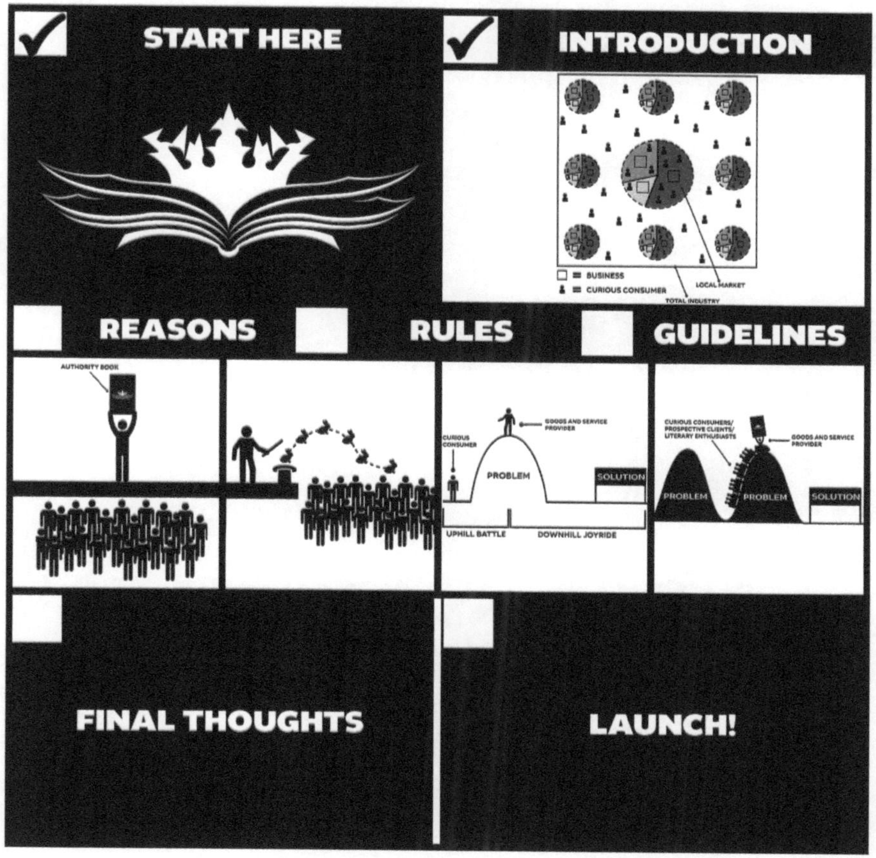

START HERE
INTRODUCTION
BUSINESS
CURIOUS CONSUMER
LOCAL MARKET
TOTAL INDUSTRY
REASONS
RULES
GUIDELINES
AUTHORITY BOOK
CURIOUS
CONSUMER
GOODS AND SERVICE
PROVIDER
PROBLEM
SOLUTION
UPHILL BATTLE
DOWNHILL JOYRIDE
CURIOUS CONSUMERS/
PROSPECTIVE CLIENTS/
LITERARY ENTHUSIASTS
GOODS AND SERVICE
PROVIDER
PROBLEM
PROBLEM
SOLUTION
FINAL THOUGHTS
LAUNCH!

SECTION II:

WHY EVERY SERIOUS ENTREPRENEUR NEEDS ONE

REASON #1: BRAND & IDENTITY

Question: How much do companies, on average, spend on Super Bowl ads?

➜ **Answer: Millions.**

Question: How much do companies, on average, make from Super Bowl ads?

➜ **Answer: More millions.**

Question: Why doesn't every company buy a Super Bowl ad then?

➜ **Answer: Because it costs millions.**

The truth is, at a certain level, marketing, branding, and client acquisition become less about secret tactics…and more about dominance. Big companies win because they can outspend the competition 1000x over. Think of the biblical story of David vs. Goliath. Most businesses are David in this story…

There is always someone bigger, badder, and meaner in the market who can outspend you, outrecruit you, and outsell you…1000x over.

So you need to play differently. If you cannot outspend them, you need to allocate your precious dollars…wisely.

What if I told you that there was an asset that could retain value, sell **FOR** you, and positively impact all potential clients, whether they decided to do business with you or not?

It might not be a Super Bowl ad, but in this case…that's Goliath's weapon. All we need is a sling and a stone.

THE SLING, THE STONE, AND THE SHEPHERD

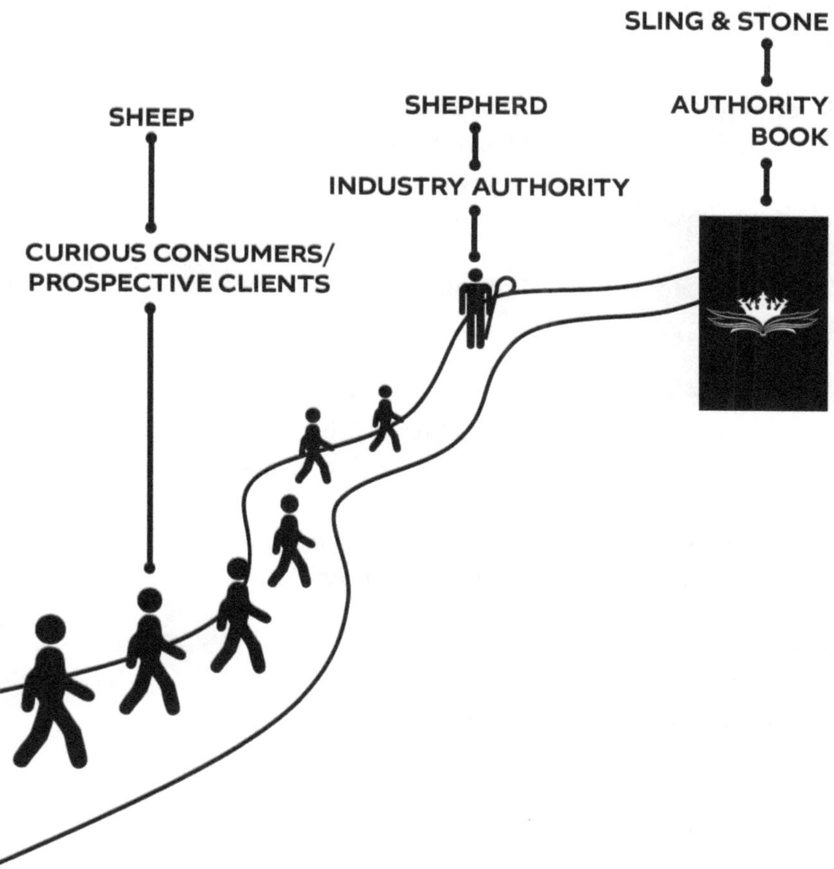

FIGURE 3: You, as the goods and service provider, are the shepherd in your industry. The curious consumers/prospective clients are the sheep. Your **Authority Book** is your sling & the value hidden within is your stone. An **Authority Book** allows you to have conversations at scale. By increasing the # of conversations, you can increase the probability of winning **The Battle for Total Market Share**.

The sling is the **Authority Book**. It's necessary, but merely a tool for launching what's really important: *the stone.*

Think of the stone as the internal contents of your book. The density, strength, and power of the stone are proportional to the value contained *within* the book...and the business/brand/business owner *behind* the book.

Furthermore, the "impact" describes the delivery of this value to any/all clients who would find it **VALUABLE**.

This is a small yet critical distinction.

Take this book, for example. Is it valuable to *every* entrepreneur? Probably not.

After all, some entrepreneurs have Goliath-sized marketing budgets. So they don't necessarily need to be efficient...because they can just throw their size around and win most of **The Battles for Market Share**.

But is this book valuable for entrepreneurs who **DON'T** have a multi-million dollar marketing budget? Abso-freakin-lutely.

Which leads me to my point...

Same internal contents. Different valuations.

Not because there is variance among the print copies of the book, but because there is variance among the prospective client base.

So if you don't want to be like most authors, you need to be intelligent about how you craft your book. Otherwise, the only person who will find it valuable...is you.

Marketing, branding, and client acquisition 101 centers around communicating with your target audience...effectively, efficiently, and ethically.

> → **If your current marketing/branding/client acquisition efforts are ineffective, you can't build your business.**

→ **If your current marketing/branding/client acquisition efforts are inefficient, you can't dominate your entire industry without breaking the bank.**
→ **If your current marketing/branding/client acquisition efforts are unethical, you're in trouble.**

A well-crafted **Authority Book** not only avoids these issues but also eliminates them altogether.

And here's the best part…

Unlike David, with 6, 9, or 12 months of work…you can construct a sling and stone…with **INFINITE** (by now, I hope you know I'm referring to my other book series) shots.

One well-crafted book with a fixed cost (varies depending on the package).

INFINITE conversations with unlimited potential revenue (varies depending on the skill of the business owner/author).

It doesn't get much better than that.

The marketplace is full of clients looking for someone to solve their problem. In this example, they are the sheep. And you, the goods and services provider, are the shepherd.

Your job is to guide them to an effective solution and to do so efficiently and ethically.

Assuming you are already effective and ethical, my job is to make your marketing, branding, and client acquisition efforts more efficient.

Rather than relying solely on your 1-on-1 time and availability, my goal is to help you construct an asset that will market for you while you spend time with your family, run your business, and enjoy the sweet satisfaction of watching your competitors' faces drop in shock as you win **The Battles for Local and Total Market Share**…effectively, efficiently, and ethically.

SECTION II OVERVIEW: THE THREE REASONS

There are three primary reasons why every serious entrepreneur needs an **Authority Book.**

Each chapter in this section will make them easy for you to understand… and most importantly, easy for you to integrate any/all corresponding strategies into your writing process.

And I cannot emphasize my previous statement enough…

There are authors.
Then there are authors with author-ity.

There. Is. A. Difference.

Writing a book isn't enough. It may impress the people around you, but prioritize your business over your ego. Otherwise, you will be an author. But one *without* authority. And what's the point of writing a book if it is ineffective?

CORE TAKEAWAY: Your book **MUST** be well-crafted.

There is nuance, skill, and strategy involved. Proceed accordingly.

With that said, this chapter focuses on the first primary reason: brand & identity.

To further expand, I'll phrase it like this:

1. **Authority Books, if well-crafted, allow you to extend the reach, intensify the impact, and amplify the communication of both your business brand and personal identity…effectively, efficiently, and ethically.**

To deconstruct the previous statement into tactical pieces of wisdom you can steal, we are going to briefly cover three things:

→ **The Reach & Supply Constraint**
→ **The Magical Art of Writing, Printing, and Publishing**

→ **Why A Book Tells You Everything You Need To Know**

Without further delay, let the magic begin…

THE REACH & SUPPLY CONSTRAINT

To keep it simple:

→ **There are millions of potential clients to reach.**
→ **There is only one of you.**

This is typically the issue with small and medium-sized businesses. Unless you're a billion-dollar conglomerate that doesn't necessarily need to sell expertise…

YOU. HAVE. TO. MARKET. YOURSELF.

You are the expert.
You are the goods and service provider.
You are the product.

And clients are begging for someone in **YOUR** industry to deliver.

If it's not you, then it **WILL** be someone else.

The market waits for no one.

Supply and demand oscillate day after day, month after month, year after year…and these oscillations mark the continuous exchange of goods and services for money.

The issue, as I said earlier, is that there is a limited supply of the product: **YOU.** As an entrepreneur, you're not just delivering goods and services. You have to recruit and train talent. You have to put out fires. You have to shake hands, kiss babies, and do everything you can to keep the wheels of your business turning…

Because if you stop, the whole thing may catch fire and burn down, thus eliminating countless jobs, which would cause problems for all who depend on you.

That's the hidden burden of being in charge. Everyone wants to be the boss, but very few want the responsibility, pressure, and criticism that come with it.

But you do…

So we need to quit complaining and start solving problems. Starting with this one:

REACH.

Assuming you are already good at having conversations (which is essentially sales), we need to extend your reach.

SAID DIFFERENTLY: You are the messenger. And you have a message. All you need is a microphone capable of capturing and distributing your thunderous voice to all who need to hear it.

Luckily for you, I sell microphones…

THE MAGICAL ART OF WRITING, PRINTING, & PUBLISHING

FIGURE 4: *Writing* intensifies your message. *Printing* multiplies the messenger. *Publishing* amplifies the microphone. Making magic really is as easy as 1-2-3.

Now that we have labeled the problem: **LIMITED REACH.**

What's the solution? Three words.

INTENSIFY. MULTIPLY. AMPLIFY.

SAID DIFFERENTLY: We need to extend your reach, seize more territory, and dominate the market. To do so, we need to **INTENSIFY** your message, **MULTIPLY** the messenger, and **AMPLIFY** your microphone.

Comprende?

And to do so, we need to fix an issue.

You probably know how to make money.

But we need to teach you *how to make magic*.

Enter: **The Magical Art of Writing, Printing, & Publishing.**

A crash course…taught by yours truly. Let the lesson begin!

1. WRITING

Writing is a skill. Don't believe me? Go write a 150-180 page manuscript.

At some point during that process, you will run into a wall: **The Writer's Wall.**

More commonly known as *writer's block*. And it's brutal…

But if you work with me, I'll help you break those walls when they appear. So don't worry about it.

What I **DO** need you to worry about is the quality of your words. I bet most of you are skilled at verbal communication.

I need you to master the *art of written communication*. And if "master" is an extreme word, I need you to be good enough to send me, your friendly neighborhood publisher, a 100-150ish page manuscript…minimum.

Because without enough clay, I cannot help you mold your literary masterpiece…

Now, when we work together in the near future, I will prescribe a structured and simple step-by-step method for you to adhere to for 6, 9, or 12 months (depending on what timeline you select) to ensure your idea is fully fleshed out.

What I need you to do right now is write down, in about a paragraph or so, your genuine thoughts on this book, its print quality, and its value for other entrepreneurs…and go leave a review on whatever online marketplace you bought this book from.

By now, I trust you have a fair sense of how seriously I take my work. Leave an honest review of what you think about this book (so far) so that I can reach other entrepreneurs and help them feed their families, put clothes on their children's backs, and put a roof over their heads…

Don't be greedy and hoard all this wisdom to yourself. Share.

Thanks in advance,

- *Giovanni*

2. PRINTING

If writing **INTENSIFIES** your message, printing **MULTIPLIES** the messenger.

Referring back to the previous analogy, an **Authority Book** is your sling, and it contains a stone of value. **PRINTING** multiplies the total number of shots available to you, thus extending your reach.

PRINTING is what allows you to be everywhere at once.

But that's for me, your friendly neighborhood publisher, to worry about. You just focus on writing…because you're the author.

3. PUBLISHING

If writing **INTENSIFIES** your message, and printing **MULTIPLIES** the messenger…

Publishing **AMPLIFIES** the microphone.

To break through the screeching noise of all the other businesses marketing online nowadays, we need to take things…*offline.*

PUBLISHING allows you to condense your thunderous voice into a quality paperback or hardcover with digital cloth (depending on your choice) container that can be opened at the client's convenience.

While every other entrepreneur is *screaming* at the masses, you are *speaking* with them.

Volume does not equal expertise. Sometimes, the quiet conversations speak the loudest.

To conclude, master **The Magical Art of Writing…**

…and leave the **Printing and Publishing** to me.

Then you'll extend your reach and move the masses with your well-crafted message.

Once you can move the masses, you can move the markets.

And if you can move markets, you can move money.

So make magic…make money…and keep reading because it's only going to get better from here.

WHY A BOOK TELLS YOU EVERYTHING YOU NEED TO KNOW

In the last chapter, I referred to this book as my resume, proposal, and magic trick…all-in-one. To reinforce this statement, I would like to add the following sentence:

An Authority Book will tell you everything you need to know about the personal identity of the author and the business brand he/she represents.

An **Authority Book** is, in a very real sense, an extension of your brand and identity. It communicates who you are both directly and indirectly.

Let me explain…

Direct communication refers to the obvious things…

- → **The words on the pages**
- → **The CTAs (call to action) sprinkled throughout the book**
- → **The images on the pages**
- → **And so on and so forth…**

Hence, why I referred to the book as my business card, resume, and proposal…

But why did I call it a magic trick?

Usually, magicians never reveal their secrets. But I did. I explicitly told you my hidden agenda. I showed you my hand. And I told you that it would still work because…

It's genuine.

It's effective.

It's science, art, and magic…wrapped into one literary masterpiece.

Which leads me to indirect communication.

Indirect communication refers to the subtle things…

→ The *font* of the words on the pages
→ The *precise insertions* of the CTAs sprinkled throughout the book
→ The *quality* of the images on the pages
→ And so much more...

Essentially, by creating this book, I am allowing you, the prospective client, the opportunity to analyze the product and inspect its quality for yourself...

At your speed, at your convenience, wherever you want...however you want...whenever you want.

Inevitably, a reader will be able to extract various details about both me (the author) and my brand (AUTHORITY BOOK LAUNCH), such as:

→ **Attention to detail**
→ **Work ethic**
→ **Sense of humor (maybe?)**
→ **Articulate (to a certain degree)**
→ **Committed to delivering value (hopefully, we'll check the reviews you all leave and see if I succeed)**
→ **And above all...aptitude, credibility, and capability.**

See, by you holding this book, you know I can deliver on the promise I am making to you: that I can make one for you and your business, too, if you'd like.

Because I backed my **intangible** promise...with **tangible** proof.

Call it science. Call it art. Call it magic.

It works.

And if it worked for me, it can work for you, too.

CONCLUSION: THE FIRST REASON

Remember:

Authority Books, if well-crafted, allow you to extend the reach, intensify the impact, and amplify the communication of both your business brand and personal identity…effectively, efficiently, and ethically.

An **Authority Book** allows you to take **The Three I's**…

1. **Impact** - *Describes what you do for others.*
2. **Income** - *Describes what is given in exchange for goods and services.*
3. **Identity** - *Describes who you become in the process.*

…and magnify the order of magnitude of *each and every one of them*.

Essentially, an **Authority Book** allows you to make magic…make money…and make a difference while doing so.

Hence, why every serious entrepreneur needs one. As in you need it by yesterday. If that's impossible, then ASAP will do.

Onto the next chapter we go…

CHAPTER SUMMARY

☑ You, as the goods and services provider, are the shepherd in your industry. The curious consumers/prospective clients are the sheep. Your **Authority Book** is your sling and the value hidden within is your stone. An **Authority Book** allows you to have conversations at scale. By increasing the number of conversations, you can increase the probability of winning **The Battle for Total Market Share**.

☑ Rather than relying solely on your 1-on-1 time and availability, my goal is to help you construct an asset that will market for you while you spend time with your family, run your business, and enjoy the sweet satisfaction of watching your competitors' faces drop in shock as you win **The Battles for Local and Total Market Share**... effectively, efficiently, and ethically.

☑ **Authority Books**, if well-crafted, allow you to extend the reach, intensify the impact, and amplify the communication of both your business brand and personal identity...effectively, efficiently, and ethically.

☑ Writing intensifies your message. Printing multiplies the messenger. Publishing amplifies the microphone. Making magic really is as easy as 1-2-3.

☑ An **Authority Book** will tell you everything you need to know about the personal identity of the author and the business brand he/she represents.

☑ Essentially, an **Authority Book** allows you to make magic...make money...and make a difference while doing so.

REASON #2:
SHOWCASE COGNITION

> *"It takes 20 years to build a reputation and five minutes to ruin it. If you think about that, you'll do things differently."*
>
> — *Warren Buffett* —

Here's the outline of the chapter:

1. **The Second Reason**
2. **The Double-Edged Sword**
3. **Clean Thinking Is Hard**
4. **Show & Tell**
5. **The Bunny In The Hat**

With that said, time is of the essence, so let's keep the pages turning.

THE SECOND REASON

Authority Books, if well-crafted, allow curious consumers/prospective clients/literary enthusiasts to see beyond the veil of the corporate brand, enter your mind, and see the way your brain works…effectively, efficiently, and ethically.

Put simply, **Authority Books** allow authors to showcase their cognition.

To define the term, cognition refers to the various mechanisms the brain uses in order to process information, including but not limited to:

- → **Thinking**
- → **Perceiving**
- → **Remembering**
- → **Problem-solving**
- → **Using language**
- → **Etc.**

It's an umbrella term for the massive, complex entity that we commonly refer to as *the brain*. Cognition is intricate, intense, and incredibly personalized.

Hence, why books are so powerful. The written word allows the author to showcase their cognition and for the readers to enter the mind of another.

With marketing, branding, and client acquisition in mind, **Authority Books** are *dangerously* powerful. The written word allows the entrepreneur to showcase their cognition—the engine that runs the business—and for readers to see beyond the veil of the corporate brand, thus being exposed (for 100-150 pages minimum) to your true personality.

In a business context, this is a weapon. A mighty sword. But it is double-edged…*which makes it dangerous if used recklessly*.

THE DOUBLE-EDGED SWORD

FIGURE 5: **Good** Authority Books *pull* curious consumers/prospective clients *towards* your business. **Bad** Authority Books *push* curious consumers/prospective clients *away* from your business. Hence, why an **Authority Book** is a double-edged sword.

As I've said time and time again before…

There are authors.
Then there are authors with author-ity.

There are books.
Then there are well-crafted books.

The reason why I repeatedly remind you of this is to set the expectations straight.

It's my responsibility, as the publisher, **to amplify your message**.

It's your responsibility, as the author, **to have a message worth amplifying in the first place.**

When you craft your book, you're creating a passageway for people to by-pass the veil of the corporate brand and peek into the way **your** mind functions and operates.

As I said before, **PUBLISHING AMPLIFIES**.

If the writing isn't well written, it can move people **AWAY** from you and your business.

See, every book is typically $30 or less. Yet, some books move the world. Others move to the back of the bookstore.

It comes down to whether you can move the reader.

To truly captivate the reader's attention, you need to showcase the way you think.

No holding back.
No pulling your punches.

And you need to do so in a way that relates to why they are there in the first place. For example, my style in this book is different from my style in my **INFINITE** books.

Why?

- → **Because the "reader" of this book is different from the "reader" of the other book.**
- → **Because the "topic" of this book is different from the "topic" of the other book.**
- → **Because the "purpose" of this book is different from the "purpose" of the other book.**

When you "showcase your cognition", you need to remember to showcase the dimension that the curious consumers/prospective clients/literary enthusiasts care about.

Otherwise, you're standing on stage speaking into the microphone as the audience is clearing out of the building, and you're losing dozens of potential customers by the second.

This book is not designed to be a textbook. ***It's a playbook***. It's a tactical guide for the busy entrepreneur.

If you reflect back across the pages you've covered, there are lines in between each idea. Most books are not formatted this way. Hence, why most books lose the reader.

We'll talk about this in greater detail in a few chapters, but for now, all you need to know is that a book is designed to increase the transparency between the reader and the author.

It's a VIP backstage pass, and your job is to hand them out like candy on Halloween.

But when doing so, make sure you're attracting ***the right type of person***. Marketing only works if it speaks to the correct demographic.

Identify your target audience and showcase the dimension of your cognition that corresponds best.

Then, be yourself. People like people.

Authority Books only work if you allow your personality to shine through the words. Don't let AI write your book for you. Respect the craft, lean into the work, and speak to the reader.

If you can do that, you're one step closer to being an author with authority.

CORE TAKEAWAY: Treat the double-edged sword with care and let the rest take care of itself.

CLEAN THINKING IS HARD

> *"Simple can be harder than complex: You have to work hard to get your thinking clean to make it simple. But it's worth it in the end because once you get there, you can move mountains."*
>
> *— Steve Jobs —*

There's a reason why writer's block is a real thing. It's difficult to **think cleanly**.

And for those of you who disagree, it's difficult to **think cleanly for a sustained period of time**.

A great book is refined down to the fine details. It's clean, fun to read, and valuable for the reader. When you write a book, you prove to the prospective client that you can think cleanly. Regardless of your profession, this simple fact is often the difference between marketing that crushes and marketing that fails.

Therefore, what better way to dominate your competition than by demonstrating to your prospective client that you can do the one thing that most people avoid doing:

THINK.

Now, from the client's perspective, the author possesses authority regarding the topic of discussion.

Once you have set the frame, you deliver. It's really simple. ***The complexity lies in the execution, not in the idea itself.***

Writing one clean page is doable with effort and revision. Writing 100-150 clean pages that blend together to create a cohesive model of thinking is quite difficult, to say the least.

But difficult problems provide outsized payoffs. Hence, why we are confronting this one head-on without any hesitation.

MID-CHAPTER GUIDED AUTHOR BONUS GIFT: SHOW & TELL

When communicating with a reader, it's critical that you, as the author, know how to show and tell. More importantly, when to do one over the other.

The title of this chapter is a CTA: showcase the way you perceive, interpret, and understand your industry. By doing so, you can create a deep psychological relationship with the reader because you are able to demonstrate your expertise, however niche or mainstream it may be, in a matter of minutes.

As far as the prospective client is concerned, they are looking for someone to solve their problems. ***Your job is to be the solution.*** That's all there is to it.

Now, as you can presumably imagine, ***telling*** them you are the solution isn't enough.

You have to **SHOW THEM.**

The best magicians don't just "tell" you how they're going to do the trick. They tell you ***what*** they're doing ***while*** they do it.

They **Show & Tell.**

Misdirection, sleight of hand, and smooth-talkin' can amaze even the brightest of minds. You don't have to learn how to make magic if you want to make money. But you do need to learn how to make magic *if you want to move people.*

Money, alone, can only take you so far. After all, let's ask the questions again:

Question: How much do companies, on average, spend on Super Bowl ads?

→ **Answer: Millions.**

Question: Why doesn't every company buy a Super Bowl ad then?

→ **Answer: Because it costs millions.**

New Question: *Why* does it cost millions?

→ **Answer: Because one creative Super Bowl ad solves all of your marketing problems—reach, effort, and potential embarrassment from putting yourself out there.**

Super Bowl ads exist as the extreme solution to three extremely painful problems:

→ **Marketing**
→ **Branding**
→ **Customer Acquisition**

Hence, why it costs millions.

But once again, unless you're a corporate conglomerate that has millions to spare, you're going to have to do the work yourself.

Why? Because you're the boss. And you're wanting to represent the top 1% of your industry, if not the top 0.1%.

You want to *show* people you are the best.

And to do that, you need to *show* people how you think.

Let the magic do the work for you. Then, as the trick is stealing their attention away, you can tell them.

One strategy from my top-secret arsenal: **Show & Tell**.

Deconstructed and made simple as a gift from me to you, one entrepreneur to another, in order to truly thank you for making it this far into the book.

If you're here, you're interested. And there's a chance we may work together in the not-so-distant future…

But for now, let's get back to the task at hand.

THE BUNNY IN THE HAT

FIGURE 6: Authors with authority make magic. How? By pulling **Belief Bunnies** out of their thinking cap, over and over again, until the reader understands you are the man/woman for the job. Typically, beliefs are personal and private. That's exactly why you are going to publicly showcase it. ***Be different. Be an outlier. Be the authority.***

Now that you know the **Show & Tell** strategy, the next natural question is:

What do you show them?

My answer: **Belief Bunnies**.

That's the magic.

I'll say it again: **Belief Bunnies**.

All you are doing, as an author, is showing them ideas that you deeply believe in. You're pulling beliefs that you deeply believe in out of your thinking cap (which we have defined as your cognition) and showing them to your audience over and over again until they finally understand that…

- → **You are the solution to their problem.**
- → **You are the authority in your industry.**
- → **You are the shepherd (goods and services provider) who can guide the lost sheep (consumers).**

And you will show them these "**Belief Bunnies**" as long as it takes for it to click that this isn't a facade. There was never any sleight of hand. This isn't a game of lies.

This is the real deal. *You are the real deal.* At least, in your respective industry. But that's all we, as entrepreneurs, need to be.

And if you are the real deal, they will inevitably realize it too. Then, a certain percentage of them will want to do business with you, and it's a win-win for…

- → **The goods and services provider (Entrepreneur)**
- → **The goods and services consumer (Client)**

Business done effectively, efficiently, and ethically. That's the game of entrepreneurship right there. It doesn't get much better than that.

See, I told you I can show you how to dominate your industry with one well-crafted book…and that is true. But for me, that's not the hard part. That's actually quite fun.

I enjoy **The Magical Art of Writing, Printing, and Publishing**.

The *real* hard part is finding authors who possess a message worth amplifying in the first place. See, I told you that if you were in the top 10% of your field in your local market, you're probably going to want an **Authority Book**.

Because it's simple…

You invest in your business and brand time and time again. And I'm merely showcasing the next investment you need to make…

However, some entrepreneurs *do not actually want* to be the authority of their industry. They do not want the pressure, criticism, and work that come along with it.

And that's okay.

But some do.

And that's okay too.

When you write your book, people will make comments. You may feel vulnerable because, at the end of the day, it's *your* words printed on paper for others to dissect.

And that's completely normal. The only thing you need to answer, for yourself, is whether the outcome is worth what it costs to get it…

Not the money or the price, but the time, energy, and effort it will take to actually make a book worth reading.

The criticism, comments, and passive-aggressive remarks will probably come from your competitors because **YOU** have an **Authority Book** and **THEY** don't.

Which, ironically, is making **THEIR** lives a lot harder because **YOU'RE** having *conversations at scale* and they…are doing it the old-fashioned way.

See, the greatest cost to this entire process is not the price, but the entrance fee.

Once you write your book, you are proceeding down a one-way path to sitting amongst the best in your respective industry.

That's definitely how most see it. And that's definitely how prospective clients see it.

Obviously, there is more to being the best than having a book with your name on it. **Show & Tell** is ineffective if the magician can't *really* do magic.

But I trust that you have handled, are handling, or will handle that for yourself. You're an effective and ethical entrepreneur, for crying out loud. It's what you do.

I'm just providing a microphone for you to **Show & Tell** everyone else… efficiently.

That's all there is to it.

CONCLUSION: THE SECOND REASON

So to summarize this entire chapter in less than 30 seconds:

Authority Books, if well-crafted, allow curious consumers/prospective clients/literary enthusiasts to see beyond the veil of the corporate brand, enter your mind, and see the way your brain works…effectively, efficiently, and ethically.

Put simply, **Authority Books** allow entrepreneurs to showcase:

- → **The engine that *drives* the business**
- → **The personality *behind* the business**
- → **And so much more…**

But what exactly are you showing & telling your curious consumers/prospective clients/literary enthusiasts?

- → **Answer: Belief Bunnies.**

You will show them ideas that you believe in over and over again until they get the message: as far as they're concerned, you're the man or woman for the job.

> → **You are the solution to their problem.**
> → **You are the authority in your industry.**
> → **You are the shepherd (goods and services provider) who can guide the lost sheep (consumers) to their ideal destination.**

Then, once you get the job…you deliver. And Bob's your uncle (if you don't know what this phrase means, look it up).

We're almost done with this section.

Only one more chapter to go…

So onwards and upwards, my fellow curious consumers/prospective clients/literary enthusiasts!

HINT: If you haven't started the next chapter yet, I suggest you turn the page. You're about 15 seconds behind. But who's counting?

CHAPTER SUMMARY

☑ **Authority Books**, if well-crafted, allow curious consumers/prospective clients/literary enthusiasts to see beyond the veil of the corporate brand, enter your mind, and see the way your brain works… effectively, efficiently, and ethically.

☑ The written word allows the entrepreneur to showcase their cognition—the engine that runs the business—and for readers to see beyond the veil of the corporate brand, thus being exposed (for 100-150 pages minimum) to your true personality.

☑ Good **Authority Books** pull curious consumers/prospective clients towards your business. Bad **Authority Books** push curious consumers/prospective clients away from your business. Hence, why an **Authority Book** is a double-edged sword.

☑ A great book is refined down to the fine details. It's clean, fun to read, and valuable for the reader. When you write a book, you prove to the prospective client that you can think cleanly. Regardless of your profession, this simple fact is often the difference between marketing that crushes and marketing that fails.

☑ The best magicians don't just "tell" you how they're going to do the trick. They tell you what they're doing while they do it. They **Show & Tell.**

☑ Misdirection, sleight of hand, and smooth talkin' can amaze even the brightest of minds. You don't have to learn how to make magic if you want to make money. But you do need to learn how to make magic if you want to move people.

☑ Authors with authority make magic. How? By pulling **Belief Bunnies** out of their thinking cap, over and over again, until the reader understands you are the man/woman for the job. Typically, beliefs are personal and private. That's exactly why you are going to publicly showcase them.

☑ Be different. Be an outlier. Be the authority.

REASON #3: PREDICT FUTURE BEHAVIOR

In the context of organic marketing, branding, and client acquisition…

…business cards, websites, logos, and unrelatable commercials no longer cut it.

The game has evolved.

And it belongs to those who know how to connect with the person *behind* the screen.

The third and final reason why every serious entrepreneur needs an **Authority Book** is simple:

Authority Books, if well-crafted, allow the curious consumer/prospective client/literary enthusiast to enthusiastically calculate the probability of their problem being solved by you and your business…effectively, efficiently, and ethically.

If it's not clear, the calculations should lean more "**YES IT WILL BE SOLVED**" than "**NO IT WON'T BE SOLVED**." Hence, the presence of the word "enthusiastically."

See, your client is coming to you, the goods and services provider, because they need you to help them solve a problem. They need a result. And oftentimes, they needed it yesterday.

And the only reason why they haven't already solved the problem is:

1. **They don't know what the problem is.**
2. **They know the problem,** *but they don't know the solution.*
3. **They know the problem, they know the solution,** *but they don't know how to implement said solution.*
4. **They know the problem, they know the solution, and they know how to implement said solution…***but they want someone else to handle it for them.*

These four conditions are what fundamentally drive commerce and the exchange of goods and services for money.

Let's use a classic elementary business model to drive this idea home: lemonade stands.

1. **A neighbor is on a run on a hot summer day, but they haven't realized they are thirsty…*yet.***
2. ***15 minutes later…*theyrealize they forgot their water (PROBLEM) and aren't sure whether to turn back or keep running.**
3. ***But then…*theysee your lemonade stand (SOLUTION).**
4. **At this point, they could either go back home to get a drink, keep running in the heat, or stop to buy a glass of lemonade.**

It's not that complicated. So when you create your organic marketing asset, **The Authority Book**, don't make it complicated.

Make it simple.

You have a business that can solve your client's problem(s). And you just want them to know that. But in order *for* them to know that, you need to *connect* with them…

The "connection" I mentioned earlier is simply describing the process of creating an intent to purchase. The "connection" describes the moment where your marketing vehicle (billboard, commercial, or in this case…an **Authority Book**) successfully boards and transports your prospective client to the destination: the solution.

Remember, they have a problem, and they want *someone* to solve it for them.

I'll say that again:

Your clients have a problem.

And your job as an entrepreneur is simple: ***deliver the solution.***

But if it was that easy, the game wouldn't be fun…now would it?

The issue is you have to convince the consumer that **YOU** are legitimately capable of delivering the solution. And you have to do so…at scale.

At this point, it's a question of aptitude and magnitude.

You need to convince **EVERY POTENTIAL CLIENT** (magnitude) of your effectiveness, efficiency, and ethics (aptitude, authority, and integrity) within the pages of a single book.

All they need is for **SOMEONE** to…

- **Solve their problem for them**
- **Show them how to solve it themselves**
- **Point the way to someone who knows how to do one of the two aforementioned activities**

Your job, when writing your book, is to replace that vague **"SOMEONE"** with your brand/business/name…in their minds…and reassure them that that is the right decision to make over and over again until they can "enthusiastically calculate the probability of their problem being solved by you and your business…effectively, efficiently, and ethically."

Now, we're transitioning away from marketing and into sales, but the fundamental issue remains the same: the consumer needs to be reassured that **YOU** are the man or woman for the job.

And you need a method of reassuring the curious consumers…but one that scales without constant 1-on-1 attention.

In addition, you need to solve this problem better, faster, and smoother with **MORE** prospective clients before your competition can even count to 10. **The Battle for Market Share** is won by those who are swift, smooth, and everything in between.

Enter: **The Authority Book.**

Typically, businesses hire sales reps (setters and closers) to solve this problem. You may have a sales division, or you may sell clients yourself in your day-to-day operations of running your business.

Regardless, in the context of the **Authority Book,** the responsibility of selling yourself and your brand…for better or for worse…falls on you.

An **Authority Book** is an asset of value. You, as the founder or entrepreneur, hold the responsibility to speak to the prospective client about **YOUR BUSINESS**. After all, you're the boss.

But fear not, because I have a plan…

For you to do so successfully, you need to follow this simple instruction: ***prove it.***

See, amateurs think sales is about deceitful manipulation. But the experts know that it's about ***transparent communication.***

If a client walks into a dealership and the salesman says they have a limited model of the ***exact*** car the client is looking for, and the client says,

"No way, there are only three in the world! You don't have one here."

The salesman, in that moment, has three choices:

1. **Waste time, energy, and words trying to convince them of a certain version of reality.**
2. **Shut up, get up, and prove it.**
3. **Sit there twiddling your thumbs while the client stares blankly at your face, waiting for you to admit you're a fraud.**

My suggestion is the second option.

Proof. Is. Everything.

When writing your book, don't reinvent the wheel.

Write a manuscript that shocks the prospective clients with an **ENORMOUS** amount of wisdom, personality, and industry-specific value.

Then, adhere to the aforementioned philosophy and let the rest take care of itself.

In publishing, after you've written your manuscript and the publisher has worked his/her magic, you will typically receive a "proof copy" of your book.

It's just a system for you to ensure the quality of the product is to your liking before we proceed to the production and publication stages.

It's the moment where your manuscript…***becomes a book***. And it's amazing.

I love receiving a proof copy of my book because it's tactile and tangible. It's proof that my message is real. In other words, it's ***reassurance***.

Your clients need ***reassurance*** that their **SOLUTION** is real. They want to know the solution…to the impossible problem they are dealing with… exists.

And it's your job to prove that it does. If your **Authority Book** fails to do so, it's not an **Authority Book**. It's a regular ol' book.

And here at **Authority Book Launch**, we don't make regular ol' books.

So focus up, and allow me to end this section in style.

Here's the outline for this chapter…

1. **The Proof Copy**
2. **The Questions of Authority**
3. **The Roadmap to Resolution**
4. **The Three I's**

Without further delay, let's begin.

THE PROOF COPY

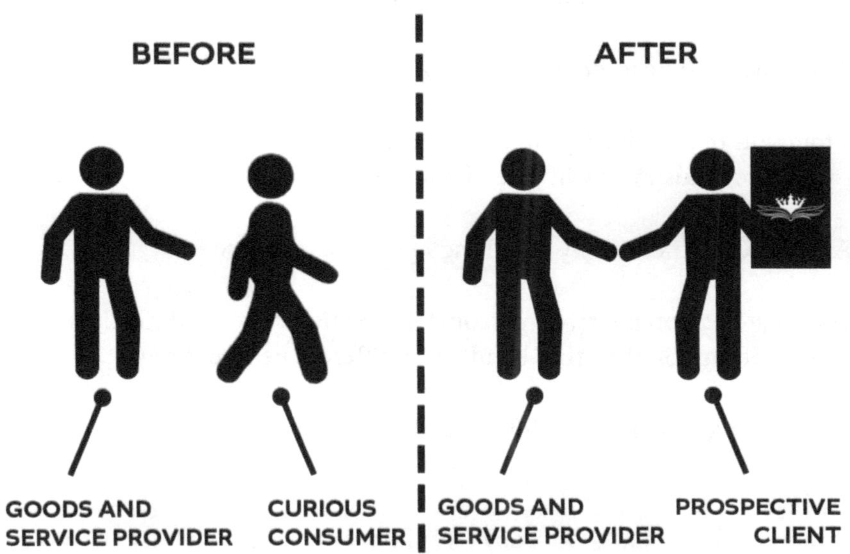

FIGURE 7: Think of your **Authority Book** as *proof* of verification. If well-crafted, the book can streamline trust and transparency while simultaneously strengthening your previously unsupported claim that you are who you say you are. How many of your competitors are willing to do the same? A little bit of extra effort goes a long way. When your prospective clients are delivered a proof copy *before* they become your clients, they are able to enthusiastically visualize the future that will occur *after* they become your clients.

Think of your **Authority Book** as your "proof copy." No, not the one publishers receive. The one entrepreneurs use to sell prospective clients who need a little bit more reassurance than the rest of them.

The **Authority Book** is not a frivolous purchase. It is a luxury investment.

It provides "proof" that you are who you say you are. By the end of reading your **Authority Book**, the prospective client should have to make up reasons why they do not want to work with you specifically.

That's the goal: *be undeniably exceptional.*

I told you the **Authority Book** will help you seize more territory in your respective industry. It will extend your reach.

At that point, there's only one thing left to do: *own it.*

For most entrepreneurs, in-person conversations are not difficult. Written conversations, on the other hand, are a different beast entirely.

Written language transcends time and space. Written language moves people.

When crafting your "proof copy", it is imperative that you pack in so much value that your credibility, integrity, and authority cannot be questioned.

Nevertheless, there will occasionally be people who **WILL** question these things.

Your job is to close those people.

Your job, when writing, is to pull as many **Belief Bunnies** out of your thinking hat as necessary. Trick after trick, bunny after bunny, belief after belief until the reader has a hard time questioning your:

- → **Credibility**
- → **Integrity**
- → **Authority**

This is your "proof" copy. This is where you prove to every curious consumer/prospective client/literary enthusiast that you are among the very best in your field.

This is where you prove to every reader that you are the man or woman for the job.

This is where you reassure the consumer over and over again until they can't help but feel an overwhelming amount of enthusiasm when they think about doing business with you.

This is where you, as the shepherd, guide the sheep to their ideal destination.

This is where you, as the goods and services provider, guide the consumer to their ideal solution.

This is where you seize territory, assume authority, and win **The Battles for Local & Total Market Share** in your industry.

By now, I hope I have drilled a crystal clear sense of responsibility into your brain. You wanted to be the authority in your field? So be it. Then write from that place.

It'll make the process much easier when we work together.

However, as you may presumably imagine, it's never that easy.

Despite your relentless effort, meticulous refinement, and ingenious brilliance...***people will question everything about you***.

Then again, if it were easy...it wouldn't be as fun now, would it?

THE QUESTIONS OF AUTHORITY

There are three fundamental questions anyone can use to destabilize your claim and proposal.

1. **Can you solve the problem effectively? Essentially, questioning your credibility or aptitude.**
2. **Can you solve the problem efficiently? Essentially, questioning your authority in the field.**
3. **Can you solve the problem ethically? Essentially, questioning your integrity.**

Now here's the important part to remember. If a reader is asking these questions, it's a good thing! Because if you legitimately are who you say you are, you have nothing to hide, so you have nothing to fear!

The issue becomes if you are not capable of solving the problem…effectively, efficiently, and ethically. In which case, **at the very worst**, you're a fraud and, **at the very best**…you're not the authority in your field.

My advice is to fix these issues **before** coming to work with me because, as I have repeatedly mentioned, I can deliver the microphone and help you hone your message. **I cannot, however, fix the messenger.** That is your responsibility.

Assuming these issues do not exist, then good news: you already are an authority in your field!

Now you just need to prove it to the reader. The easiest way to do that is to **confront their questions head-on.** They're only asking the natural questions.

Some entrepreneurs would take offense because their ego cannot stand when a prospective client questions their authority. **Don't be that entrepreneur.**

Some entrepreneurs would be impatient because their attention span cannot concentrate when a client questions their authority for a significant amount of time. **Don't be that entrepreneur.**

If a client is asking questions, it implies one of these things:

- → **They are curious.**
- → **They are concerned.**
- → **They require reassurance.**
- → **They are genuinely trying to irritate you.**

Regardless, all four types of customers are normal. Your job is to write a single manuscript that serves all four.

This is the difficult part. Fortunately, you now know a 23-year-old (at the time of writing this book) publisher who knows how to deal with these types of issues.

So don't fret.

If they are asking these questions, it typically means they need reassurance.

Enter: **The Roadmap to Resolution.**

THE ROADMAP TO RESOLUTION

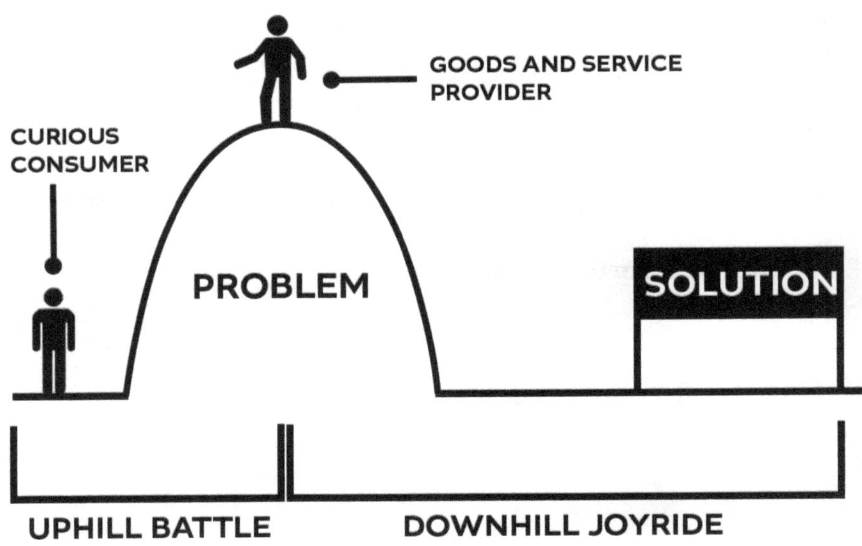

FIGURE 8: As the goods and service provider, you possess the solution to your prospective client's problems. But as the author, your job is to help them *endure* the uphill battle that precedes the downhill joyride to resolution. Said differently, no one cares about the **Authority Author's** message (the uphill battle). They care about what comes *after* consuming the message (the downhill joyride to resolution). Write accordingly.

This singular concept, if executed correctly, should answer all of the questions mentioned earlier.

When a client is questioning your aptitude, integrity, and authority, it is your job to direct them to **The Roadmap to Resolution**. Once on the road, you can reassure them as you guide them to their ideal solution.

Shepherds don't lose their cool when a sheep wanders. *They guide.* It is their responsibility.

Similarly, your job is to guide without being impatient, angry, frustrated, irritated, or any of the other human emotions that may arise when dealing with curious consumers/prospective clients/literary enthusiasts.

To clarify this point, take a look at the contents of my **Authority Book**. The further along a reader goes in the book, the more gifts they receive.

As they are receiving gifts and walking towards the ideal destination (which we have defined as having their own **Authority Book**), I am simply reassuring them by throwing so much undeniable proof at them that I possess the aptitude, integrity, and authority required to deliver the solution... effectively, efficiently, and ethically.

Some readers were committed to working with me within the first 10 pages. Others need more reassurance. Some readers never planned on working with me at all; they are just reading to find as much knowledge as they can before going elsewhere.

Either way, it doesn't matter. I wrote this manuscript for *each and every type* of curious consumer.

See, when writing, the mistake most authors make is that they hide their wisdom. You have to be generous, otherwise the world won't know you had any to begin with.

The secret is to know *what wisdom to give* the client to implement, and *what wisdom to keep secret* for **YOU** to implement as the goods and services provider.

After all, you run a business, and you are the authority in your industry.

Therefore, there are certain activities and problems that only you/your business/your brand can solve.

That's the game. As readers read this book, they are following my **Roadmap to Resolution**. Some will attempt to leave the road once they feel like they have stolen enough value, and that is okay.

I, as the author, believe in my aptitude, integrity, and authority in this industry. The **Proof Copy** exists to reassure those readers that even if they decide to leave for now, the destination (**AUTHORITYBOOKLAUNCH. COM**) will always be available for them if/when they are ready.

You, as the entrepreneur, need to own the territory and reassure the clients that you are the man or woman for the job…as many times as necessary for them to feel calm, collected, and energetically enthusiastic.

Once you progress far enough down the road, you reach into your pocket and unlock the gate. You showcase your solution, deliver the solution to a certain percentage of the readers, and guarantee customer satisfaction.

GUARANTEE THE FINAL COPY'S QUALITY

When you are having conversations at scale, the important part is to make sure the readers know…not only do you possess the aptitude, integrity, and authority required to solve their problem…but you also are willing to guarantee they will be happy with the final copy.

Imagine the prospective client most entrepreneurs are afraid of: the one who, regardless of how much proof you throw at them, still needs constant reassurance.

When these clients arise, I deploy the following solution: **"The Reassurance Roller Coaster."**

THE REASSURANCE ROLLERCOASTER

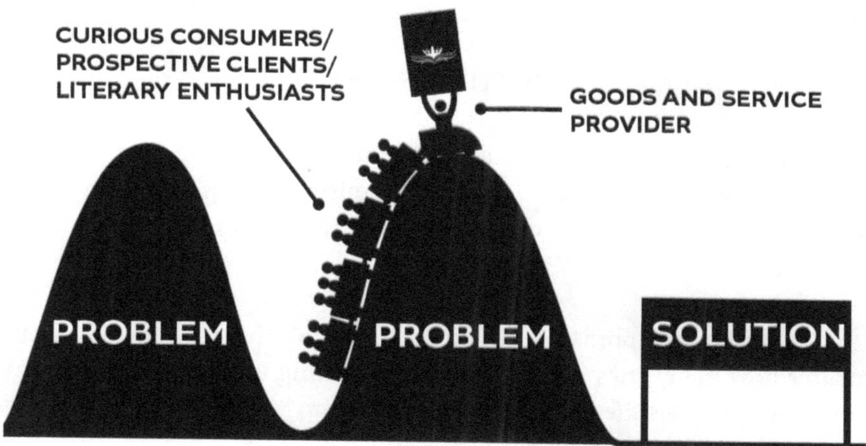

FIGURE 9: Some prospective clients need more reassurance than others. Your job, as the goods and service provider, is to provide it *generously*. When writing, write for the prospective client who needs *the most* reassurance. If you can do that, without getting impatient, angry, frustrated, irritated, or any of the other human emotions that may arise when dealing with curious consumers/prospective clients/literary enthusiasts...your **Authority Book** will thrive.

Imagine a child who has never ridden a roller coaster in their life. Would you expect them to be throwing their hands up and screaming with total joy and excitement as their life flashes before their eyes?

Absolutely not.

Are some kids willing to be like that on their first roller coaster ride?

Absolutely.

But if some kids are genuinely scared, concerned, or worried about their safety during the roller coaster ride…that's alright too.

It's your job to **GUARANTEE THEIR SAFETY**.

In business, the easiest way to do this is to guarantee the final outcome matches the quality expectations of the consumer. This way, they know that they will be well taken care of, even if **The Road to Resolution** gets a little bumpy.

As a publisher, my phrase is "The final copy is all that matters." It doesn't matter how many tries it takes; you keep pushing until the quality of the final copy matches the expectation of the author.

Your job, as an entrepreneur, is to provide "**The Reassurance Roller Coaster**" to every reader as you carry them down **The Road to Resolution**.

If you can do that, without being impatient, angry, frustrated, irritated, or any of the other human emotions that may arise when dealing with curious consumers/prospective clients/literary enthusiasts…your **Authority Book** will thrive.

Otherwise, you are eliminating the quality of the launch before it has even begun.

Here's why: ***readers leave reviews.***

The reason why **FRAUDS** should not write an **Authority Book** is that…

1. **Authority Books, if well-crafted, allow you to extend the reach, intensify the impact, and amplify the communication of both your business brand and personal identity...**
2. **Authority Books, if well-crafted, allow curious consumers/ prospective clients/literary enthusiasts to see beyond the veil of the corporate brand, enter your mind, and see the way your brain works...**
3. **Authority Books, if well-crafted, allow curious consumers/ prospective clients/literary enthusiasts to enthusiastically calculate the probability of their problem being solved by you and your business...**

And if you lack the aptitude, integrity, or authority **BEFORE** writing the book, you're not going to magically have it **AFTER** writing the book. The readers **WILL** figure it out, and *they will tell everyone.*

Hence, why I referred to **Authority Books** as **Double-Edged Swords**.

They can, if well-crafted, build your authority and help you dominate your entire industry...

But they can also, if terribly crafted, destroy your authority and ruin your reputation across the industry.

Authority Books are designed to provide transparency, proof, and clarity as to **WHO** you, as the author, are.

If you possess the aptitude, integrity, and authority *you claim to possess...* the sky's the limit.

If not, then good luck!

CONCLUSION: THE THIRD REASON

Authority Books, if well-crafted, allow the consumer to enthusiastically calculate the probability of their problem being solved by you and your business...effectively, efficiently, and ethically.

The strategies within this section are merely a few words of wisdom for you, the aspiring **Authority Author**, to heed before beginning your journey.

This section answers:

WHY EVERY SERIOUS ENTREPRENEUR NEEDS AN AUTHORITY BOOK.

The next section offers some tactical rules of thumb to consider when working on your literary project. Consider it yet another set of **BONUS GIFTS** for still reading.

Question: How many readers make it past the first chapter of a book?

→ **Answer: Around 10%.**

You've just concluded the **SECOND SECTION** of this book. So be proud, and enjoy the rest of the roller coaster ride!

See you in the next section…

CHAPTER SUMMARY

☑ In the context of organic marketing, branding, and client acquisition…business cards, websites, logos, and unrelatable commercials no longer cut it.

☑ **Authority Books**, if well-crafted, allow the curious consumer/prospective client/literary enthusiast to enthusiastically calculate the probability of their problem being solved by you and your business…effectively, efficiently, and ethically.

☑ You need to convince EVERY POTENTIAL CLIENT (magnitude) of your effectiveness, efficiency, and ethics (aptitude, authority, and integrity) within the pages of a single book.

☑ Think of your **Authority Book** as proof of verification. If well-crafted, the book can streamline trust and transparency while simultaneously strengthening your previously unsupported claim that you are who you say you are. How many of your competitors are willing to do the same? A little bit of extra effort goes a long way. When your prospective clients are delivered a proof copy before they become your clients, they are able to enthusiastically visualize the future that will occur after they become your clients.

☑ As the goods and services provider, you possess the solution to your prospective client's problems. But as the author, your job is to help them endure the uphill battle that precedes the downhill joyride to resolution. Said differently, no one cares about the **Authority Author's** message (the uphill battle). They care about what comes after consuming the message (the downhill joyride to resolution). Write accordingly.

☑ Some prospective clients need more reassurance than others. Your job, as the goods and services provider, is to provide it generously. When writing, write for the prospective client who needs the most reassurance. If you can do that without getting impatient, angry, frustrated, irritated, or any of the other human emotions that may arise when dealing with curious consumers/prospective clients/literary enthusiasts…your **Authority Book** will thrive.

THE ROADMAP

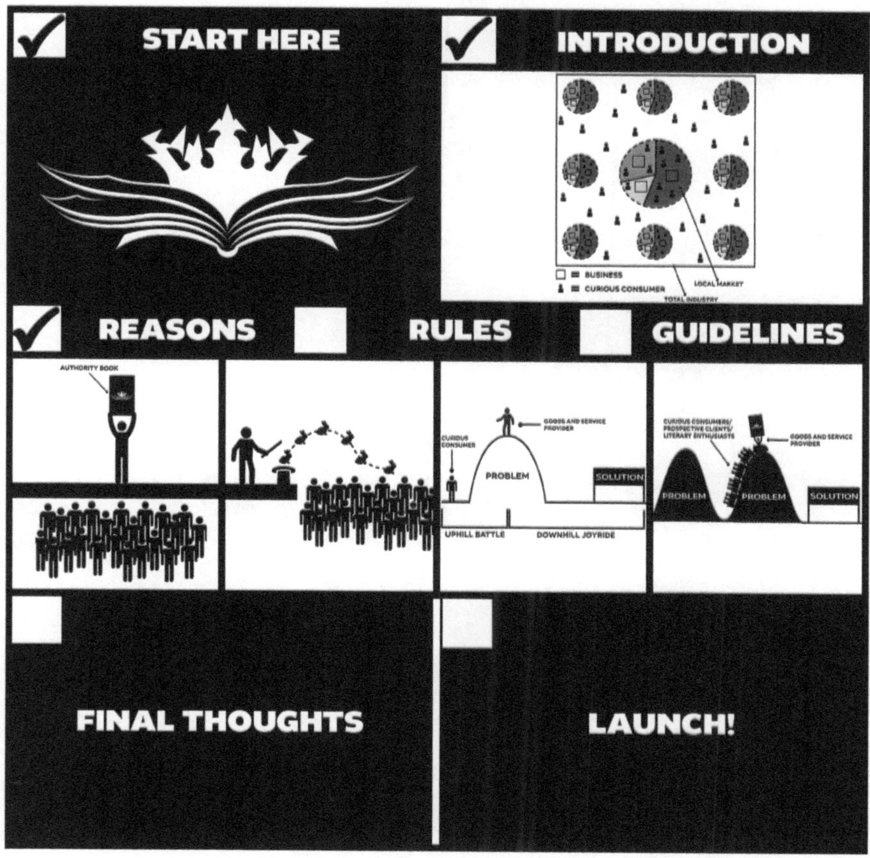

START HERE
INTRODUCTION
BUSINESS
CURIOUS CONSUMER
LOCAL MARKET
TOTAL INDUSTRY
REASONS
RULES
GUIDELINES
AUTHORITY BOOK
CURIOUS CONSUMER
GOODS AND SERVICE PROVIDER
PROBLEM
SOLUTION
UPHILL BATTLE
DOWNHILL JOYRIDE
CURIOUS CONSUMERS/ PROSPECTIVE CLIENTS/ LITERARY ENTHUSIASTS
GOODS AND SERVICE PROVIDER
PROBLEM
PROBLEM
SOLUTION
FINAL THOUGHTS
LAUNCH!

SECTION III:

TACTICAL RULES OF THUMB

RULE #1: THE READER IS ALWAYS RIGHT

> *"Quality in a service or product is not what you put into it. It is what the client or customer gets out of it."*
>
> — *Peter Drucker* —

SECTION III OVERVIEW

By now, I trust you know **WHY EVERY SERIOUS ENTREPRENEUR NEEDS AN AUTHORITY BOOK.**

Moving forward, this section will discuss…

- → **Some of the main mistakes most entrepreneurs make when writing their book…**
- → **Why it costs them time, money, and energy they can't get back…**
- → **And most importantly, how you can avoid The Tragedy of The Author altogether…**

And the next section has more bonus stuff for those who stick around…

Sound good?

Now, each chapter of this section will cover a tactical rule of thumb for you to keep in mind when writing your **Authority Book.**

Obviously, I will share more with you when we work together. For now, I figured I'd get the ball rolling so you don't finish this book empty-handed…

Starting with…

RULE #1: THE READER IS ALWAYS RIGHT

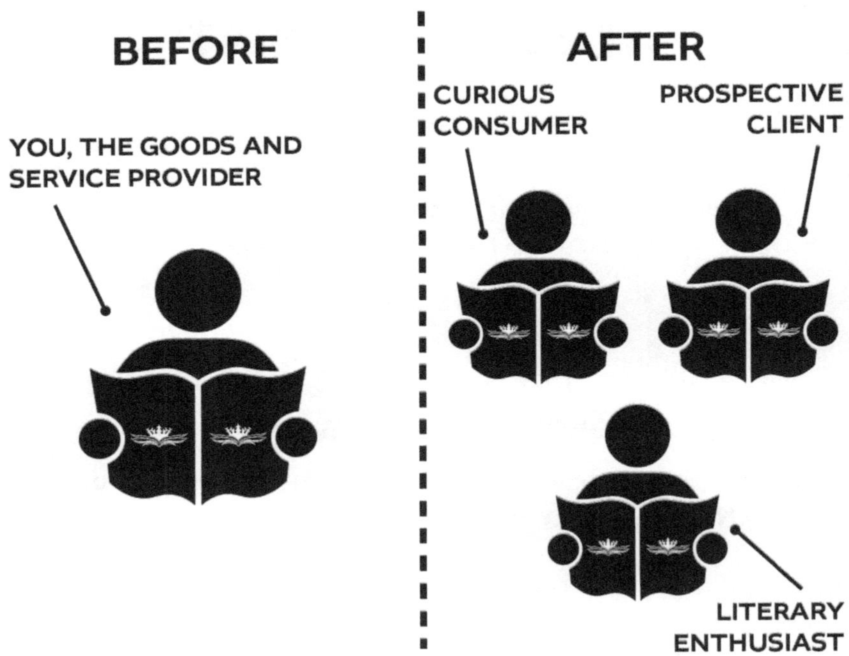

FIGURE 10: Write your **Authority Book** for your ideal reader. Make it fun, entertaining, **and** transformative. By the time they've finished reading your book, the ones who **really** want the solution should be **pounding** on your door enthusiastically, ready to exchange dollars for your goods and services. Then you deliver, make them happy, and it's a win-win scenario for everyone. The beautiful game of entrepreneurship. Easy as 1-2-3.

There are authors.
Then there are authors with author-ity.

Generally, authors who write for themselves tend to have little to no authority because…(SPOILER ALERT)…***they wrote the book for themselves.***

Yes, I know it might seem counterintuitive (sarcasm, if you can't tell).

But readers can tell **WHO** the author is writing the book for.

Typically, without reading more than a page…

Think about it. Haven't you picked up a book, opened it, and immediately shut it because the words are tiny, there are no graphics, or there are 789 pages….

There's a reason why most students hate textbooks.
There's a reason why most books don't sell.

They're not written for the reader. They're written for the author.

This is typical. ***But I want you to be atypical.***

I want you to write selflessly, give generously, and think about the person **BEHIND** the book.

In the last section, we discussed how the best marketers nowadays optimize the content for the person **BEHIND** the screen.

Obviously, to a certain degree. Just because you sell accounting, HVAC, or plumbing services, it doesn't mean you need to start dancing on social media. Nonetheless, you have to be personable.

Relatable. Someone others can relax around yet still listen to. And note, I'm not talking about when you're speaking to a client in-person: you can be, do, and say whatever you want then.

However, if you want to write a book that crushes…you need to find your **WRITING VOICE.**

Most importantly, you need to find a writing voice that most readers wouldn't mind listening to for 100-150 pages...*minimum.*

Assuming that you've understood the general gist of what I am saying, let's ask the next natural question...

What does this mean in tactical-ity? (or practicality, whatever floats your boat)

STEP #1: IDENTIFY THE READER

First, you need to know who you're talking to.

- → **Who is your reader?**
- → **What is your book about, and why do they need to read it?**
- → **What makes your book unique?**
- → **Most importantly, who are they going to be AFTER reading it?**

A good **Authority Book** takes a reader from their problem to their solution.

Oftentimes, that solution is you and your business.

This isn't unethical. It's the truth.

If they were able to solve the problem themselves, they wouldn't need to read the book now, would they?

You're not reading this book because you're planning on doing all the writing, printing, and publishing work yourself. You probably would like someone to solve that problem while you continue to run your business.

Similarly, your reader is not looking to...

- → **Do their own accounting (if you're an accountant)**
- → **Adjust their own backs (if you're a chiropractor)**
- → **Edit their own videos (if you're a video editor)**
- → **Defend themselves in court (if you're a lawyer)**

If you didn't get the point, your book is a journey that your reader will take to get to his/her ideal destination: you/your business/your brand.

And this will happen to each and every single reader…if you make the journey **FOR THEM**.

- → They need to feel like you wrote the book **FOR THEM**.
- → They need to feel like you are talking directly **TO THEM**.
- → They need to feel like their solution is waiting at the end of the book **FOR THEM**.

To guarantee these outcomes occur, you have to **IDENTIFY YOUR READER**.

Specifically,

- → **Who is your reader BEFORE they read your book?**
- → **Who is your reader AFTER they read your book?**

As for the discrepancy between the two answers…well, that's where you come in.

Your role, as the author, is to craft a **Roadmap to Resolution** which will bridge the **BEFORE** version of themselves with the **AFTER** version of themselves.

The book is merely a vessel for what's truly valuable: *your voice.*

As we said earlier, the book is the shepherd's sling. And your **VOICE** is the valuable stone.

Your voice is what carries unique value. **NO ONE**, and I mean **NO ONE**, will ever think what you think, how you think it, for the exact reasons you think it…

There is a reason why literature and art are timeless and well-respected. It's because the masterpiece is, and always will be, unique to the **AUTHOR** and **ARTIST**.

I don't want you to feel like you have to go through this entire process alone. You absolutely could, if you so chose, but you'd probably waste a lot of time, energy, and effort solving problems that I could help you avoid.

I want you to **WANT** to craft your masterpiece. Then, I want you to book a call with me, and I'll guide you through the rest of the process.

That's the general idea:

- → **You are the READER with a problem.**
- → **I am the GUIDE to the solution.**

And that will be true for you when you write your book. Your future readers want you to guide them to the good stuff so they can avoid all the bad stuff.

It's really not that complicated.

STEP #2: SPEAK OUT LOUD

Once you've identified the **BEFORE** and **AFTER** versions of your reader, you need to talk to them.

Out loud.

If you have clients who you think represent the target demographic of your book, visualize them in your head when you are speaking.

Analyze **HOW** you talk to them. Is it boring? ***Probably not.*** Is it stagnant and monotone? ***Probably not.***

Identify the key details of **YOUR VOICE** and jot them down somewhere for you to refer back to.

The reason why this step is a good beginner's strategy for those of you who are not quite sure what your writing voice sounds like is that it gets you out of your own head.

Writing is similar to water. The words should flow onto the paper. To do so comfortably takes practice.

Assuming you're an effective entrepreneur, I can probably guarantee you're articulate when it comes to verbal communication in some shape, way, or form.

I want you to find your voice doing something you already know how to do:

→ **Speaking to curious consumers and prospective clients.**

Do this process with as many clients as you can think of. 5, 10, 100 if that's what it takes…

As you do so, ***you'll find that a pattern starts to emerge.*** Do as many repetitions until you start to see the pattern:

→ **"Your client voice."**

We all speak to different people in different ways. We are multifaceted creatures. I speak to my fiancée with a different voice than I do to my readers.

I'm sure you do too.

Note any distinctions between the two, and jot them down.

It'll make this next part easier.

STEP #3: SPEAK ON PAPER

Now, I want you to take the voice that you found while speaking out loud… and throw it onto the paper.

Not too complicated, right?

If/when you try this out for yourself, you'll probably find that there is a disconnect.

Some of you may kill it on the first run. Others may require a few more reps.

My message to you is: ***keep trying.***

I don't necessarily need you to figure this out right now. I just need you to trust me when I tell you ***it's possible, it's necessary, and it's worth it.***

For your readers to feel like you are genuinely speaking to them, you need to quite literally speak to them ***through the book***. I know…***shocker***.

As I told you before, you are the messenger with a message. The book is just the microphone that amplifies your voice.

Easy as 1-2-3.

CONCLUSION

These are just a handful of ideas for you to hoard, steal, or generously share with others (if you leave a review and/or share this book with other entrepreneurs).

There's plenty more that you will need later when we're working on the actual project. For now, this section will have to do.

RULE #1: The Reader is Always Right.

Onto Rule #2…

CHAPTER SUMMARY

☑ Write your **Authority Book** for your ideal reader. Make it fun, entertaining, and transformative. By the time they've finished reading your book, the ones who really want the solution should be pounding on your door enthusiastically, ready to exchange dollars for your goods and services. Then you deliver, make them happy, and it's a win-win scenario for everyone. The beautiful game of entrepreneurship. Easy as 1-2-3.

☑ Your role, as the author, is to craft a **Roadmap to Resolution** that will bridge the BEFORE version of themselves with the AFTER version of themselves.

RULE #2: PRESENTATION MATTERS

PRESENTATION. MATTERS.

Even when it seems like it doesn't, **it does**…

And in the context of a book, the way you present your ideas often matters more than the innate value of the ideas themselves.

That's the general gist of this chapter.

To further explore **this** idea, we'll cover three things:

1.   **People Love a Good Show**
2.   **Set The Stage**
3.   **Be Generous**

Let's get to it.

PEOPLE LOVE A GOOD SHOW

FIGURE 11: Presentation matters. Even when it seems like it doesn't, *it does*. And in the context of a book, the way you present your ideas often matters *more* than the innate value of the ideas themselves. When you write *your* **Authority Book**, 95% of the skill comes down to "staging" your ideas effectively.

Everyone loves to be entertained. Since the dawn of the 21st century, hundreds if not thousands of breakthrough technologies, mechanisms, and machines have been developed to **ENTERTAIN YOUR BRAIN.**

Neural stimulation is necessary, and we have become addicted to it as a society.

Being "bored" is no longer as common as it perhaps once was.

But this doesn't matter as much as what it implies: we, as a society, have a small attention span.

There's a reason why those 30-second Super Bowl ads we discussed earlier cost millions. And it's not just because of the reach.

It's because it's hard to get people to pay attention.

Especially over 100 million of them.

And that's with a 30-second video that costs millions. If these companies are putting that much effort into a video that is shorter than making popcorn in the microwave, then I suggest you buckle up because, for your **Authority Book** to legitimately be effective, you have to entertain the minds of your readers...***for an entire book.***

Tough job, I know. But it **can** be done. It **is** done...often.

And to create an asset that can position you as an industry-leading authority, you're going to need to see this job through to completion.

Fortunately, you have a tour guide who's been answering all your questions. Sometimes, questions you didn't even know you needed to ask in the first place.

Which leads me to ***this*** question:

"What's in it for me?"

That's what your readers are going to be asking…page after page…paragraph after paragraph…word after word.

And it's your job, as the author, to make sure you answer this question throughout the entire book.

People love a good show.

So give them one.

SET THE STAGE

In real estate, agents will often "stage" a home that is listed on the market to help sell it.

But why does this work?

"Staging", when done correctly, allows prospective clients to envision how a home functions.

Said differently, "staging" allows people to feel at home…before it's ***actually*** their home.

And it works.

So that's exactly what I need you to do. I told you that people love a good show.

So I need you to **SET THE STAGE**.

In the publishing world, there are two categories to think about:

1. **The Internal**
2. **The External**

Most authors believe that it's the words that matter. But the words are only part of it. The "internal staging" is what structures the words. The "external staging" is what sells the words.

In this chapter, we're going to narrow our focus to the former topic: **IN-TERNAL STAGING**.

When we work together, I will help you do this at the level required for the book to come out the way you want it to. For now, I'm merely going to introduce the idea so you know what to expect.

When you write your authority book, 95% of the skill comes down to "staging" your ideas correctly.

To draw parallels to the real estate analogy, in this context…you are the seller. I'm the agent.

It's my job to help you "stage" your ideas in a manner that is effective, efficient, and ethical.

However, seeing as I cannot write the book for you, I need you to understand enough of the idea yourself to give me enough good clay to help you mold your masterpiece.

So listen closely…

PRESENTATION. MATTERS.

I'm repeating this rule because it's arguably the most important one in this book. As I said before, 95% of writing comes down to how you "stage" the ideas. Not the ideas themselves.

Which is where most authors mess up…

There are about a million ways to present a single idea.

And that's lowballing.

When you write your chapters, you're trying to present the ideas in a manner that activates and engages the deepest parts of the brain.

To do so effectively, efficiently, and ethically requires skill. So, as a tactical rule of thumb: ***make it fun.***

Make the idea that you are explaining…*fun.*

Entertaining.

Interesting.

Fascinating.

Extraordinary.

Use whatever word you want, but the main point is…*the words you choose to include within your book should be intentional.*

A good book is merely a collection of words, strung together to effectively, efficiently, and ethically communicate a corresponding collection of ideas that are currently gathering dust in your brain.

If you think about any book, it's not the ideas that make you stay: *it's the way they are communicated.*

Said differently, it's the presentation.

It's the same thing with all forms of written language.

Most songs repeat the chorus. Over and over again. Some songs quite literally have 1-2 sentences in them…and yet we love them.

The idea doesn't need to be complicated because the idea isn't what sells. It's everything *around* the idea.

If you listen to a song, and you dislike the beat…you're probably not going to make it far enough to analyze the deep meaning behind the artist's lyrics…because the song didn't activate and engage the part(s) of your brain required to get past the first 15 seconds.

Don't be that artist.

Don't be that author.

I don't want your readers to disengage after the first page or so because it wasn't presented properly. I want your readers to make it to the end of the book.

Obviously, there will be some readers who, quite literally, are incapable of making it to the end of any book for some unknown reason.

But that's okay. Your job is to serve. Even if it's only for a chapter...*serve*.

Sometimes, the readers who don't want to read the whole book will be your greatest clients...they just didn't need as much reassurance as the rest of the group.

They loved the song after the first 15 seconds.

Your job is to prepare for all possibilities and write a book that does the same.

So take your ideas and set the stage for them to shine in the spotlight. We'll discuss this in greater detail once we've begun working on your project.

Just keep it in your back pocket for now.

BE GENEROUS

To present your ideas correctly, *you will need to be extremely generous.*

Let me explain...

You are trying to write an **Authority Book**. Not a text message. Not details that you're throwing up on a flyer or billboard. An **Authority Book**.

There's a reason *why* your customers will be impressed if/when you choose to write your **Authority Book**.

Because it's hard. It's difficult. And 99% of your competition...isn't going to do it. Which leaves an opportunity for the top 1% to show *why* they are different.

Technically, there are other publishers out there who **could** publish your book. But if they wanted to be the best in the industry, they would work harder for their prospective clients' attention.

Half of the power in the **Authority Book** is about showing who you are and how far you are willing to go to succeed in the marketplace.

For yourself, for your family, for your business, and for your clients.

Consumers and prospective clients want to know they will be taken care of. The best way to prove that…is to be generous…**before** they are your actual clients.

Authority Books are a tool you, your business, and your brand can use to achieve this objective. But a book is merely an empty vessel with blank pages.

It's a blank canvas that's waiting to be painted.

So if/when you decide to paint it, be generous. Not regarding the **quantity** of words, but regarding the **quality** of words.

Share some ideas and let the readers keep them in their back pocket. It'll let them know you are the real deal. More importantly, **they'll want more.**

Your competition only gives attention and care to people **after** they become clients.

When your clients see that you are willing to give attention and care to people **before** they become your clients, it sets the tone for how your business operates.

In the context of the book, it's your job to **give…give…and then give some more.** Writing is about service. It's about generously sharing the words, ideas, and messages with the people you want to positively impact the most.

If you can get on board with this idea, you'll have a much better experience. And a much better book.

As I have said before, you're showing all your cards…because you know you're the best.

You have to believe that. Because if you don't believe that, your readers, curious consumers, and prospective clients won't either.

If you really are the authority in your industry, you have more value to give than you can even fit in one book in the first place. Which is the whole point…

Question: What do you think the clients are going to believe when they see you gave them all this good stuff…and haven't even batted an eye?

→ **Answer: That you have plenty more where that came from.**

I've been doing it this whole time because I told you in the beginning…this is **my Authority Book**.

The best lawyers don't lose a case just because it's not the big one. *They win.*

The best agents don't care if this specific property's commission is the record-setting one. *They sell.*

The best actors don't care if this specific role is going to win them an Oscar. *They perform.*

The best in the world don't need a reason to perform. *They need a reason not to.*

I say this to you, the authority who is seeking to craft an asset of quality, so you know not to pull your punches.

Let those hands fly…

The reader wants the good stuff.
The people want a good show.

So give it to them…generously.
In abundance.

By the time they're done reading your book, their pockets should be over-flowing with ideas that they're trying to steal, memorize, or adopt.

Then they'll ask the next natural question…

"Do you happen to have more?"

And when they do, you give it to them…*after* they become a client, of course.

Win-win for everyone.

CHAPTER SUMMARY

☑ Presentation matters. Even when it seems like it doesn't, it does. And in the context of a book, the way you present your ideas often matters more than the innate value of the ideas themselves. When you write your **Authority Book**, 95% of the skill comes down to "staging" your ideas effectively.

☑ A good book is merely a collection of words, strung together to effectively, efficiently, and ethically communicate a corresponding collection of ideas that are currently gathering dust in your brain.

☑ If you think about any book, it's not the ideas that make you stay: ***it's the way they are communicated.***

☑ The idea doesn't need to be complicated because the idea isn't what sells. It's everything around the idea.

☑ To present your ideas correctly, you will need to be extremely generous.

☑ Share some ideas and let the readers keep them in their back pocket. It'll let them know you are the real deal. More importantly, they'll want more.

☑ Your competition only gives attention and care to people after they become clients. When your clients see that you are willing to give attention and care to people before they become your clients, it sets the tone for how your business operates.

☑ In the context of the book, it's your job to give…give…and then give some more. Writing is about service. It's about generously sharing the words, ideas, and messages with the people you want to positively impact the most.

RULE #3: JUDGE A BOOK BY ITS COVER

In the publishing world, there are two categories to think about:

1. **The Internal**
2. **The External**

The previous chapter discussed the former.

So this chapter will discuss the latter.

People love to say, "Don't judge a book by its cover." And I believe this is generally good advice with regard to most situations in life.

Unfortunately, it's completely disregarded once people walk into a bookstore.

Most people have judged…do judge…and will judge a book by its cover.

Do with that information what you will.

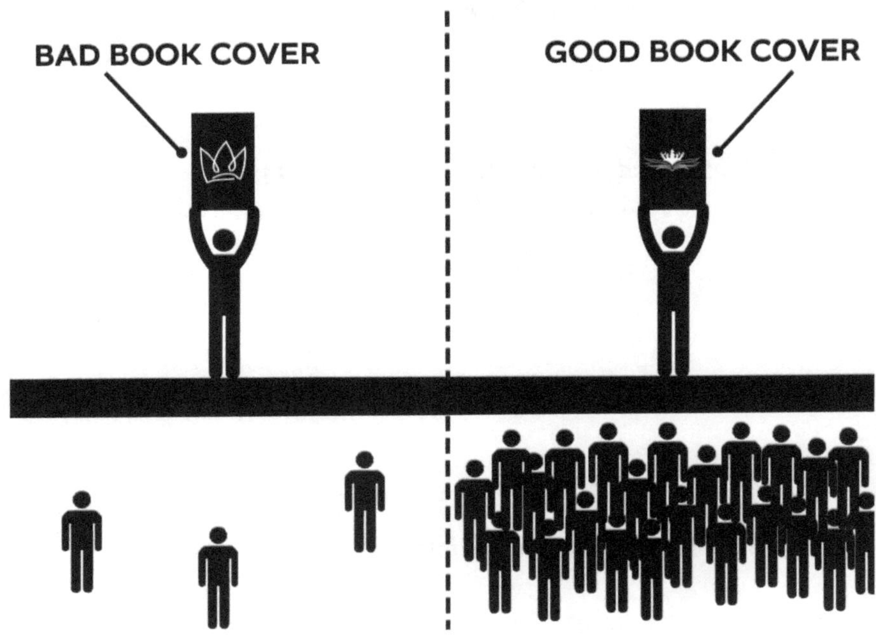

FIGURE 12: People love to say, "Don't judge a book by its cover." And I believe this is generally good advice with regard to most situations in life. Unfortunately, it's completely disregarded once people walk into a bookstore. Most people **have judged, do judge, and/or will judge a book by its cover**. Do with that information what you will.

Books are boring for most people. Said differently, most people don't like to read. It's not as fun as watching a movie, going out to eat at your favorite restaurant, or any of the other **INFINITE** things you could do *other* than reading a book.

However, people still read books. *Just the best ones.*

Most people aren't going to read 100 books a year. But they will read the 1-3 books that will either:

A) Entertain them with a story they've never heard before.
B) Educate them with the knowledge they need now more than ever.

Assuming most of you are going to lean towards the second option, the following statement is even more important for you than for the fictional authors:

→ **YOUR TOPIC MATTERS.**
→ **YOUR TITLE MATTERS.**
→ **YOUR SUBTITLE MATTERS.**
→ **YOUR BOOK COVER MATTERS.**
→ **THE EXTERNAL MATTERS.**

Read that again. Say it out loud. Do whatever you need to do to anchor it into your long-term memory.

Most people judge a book by its cover. *Even if they say they don't.*

Yes, I'm calling them liars.

Yes, you can tell them I said so.

Think about it a different way:

Let's say I cooked you a nice steak. Then I wrapped it with rotten bacon. Then I placed it in front of you with a nice, big smile across my face.

Would you instinctively, at that moment, think to yourself…

"The steak is going to taste amazing, it's just the bacon that smells bad."

Doubtful.

Most people would naturally assume that if the bacon is rotten…the steak can't possibly be much better.

Of course, the logic is flawed and not necessarily true. Nonetheless, I know I wouldn't test my chances…and I doubt you would either. Not unless you wanted to risk a long night sitting on the porcelain throne (the toilet, for those who are a bit behind).

My point is: *the wrapping matters.* Even when people try to convince you that it doesn't…

Now, when we work together, I'll take care of the cover for you. Of course, I'll collaborate with you to make sure it's derived from your creativity or vision.

When we work together, I can even help you with the title and subtitle. If that's concerning you, don't sweat it.

What I need you to do…*is nail the topic.*

See, I know my industry. I doubt I know yours as well as you do. That's why you are the authority.

So naturally, I'm going to have a hard time telling **YOU** what topic to write about.

I need you to think on this and have an answer for me *before* we meet to discuss the project.

Even if all you can come up with on your own is the general idea, that's good enough for me.

Just pick a topic that you believe your readers are dying to hear about. When I say dying, I mean…if this were the *only* book from your industry they'd ever want to read…this is the topic they would need to hear about.

Ideally, it's one that they **NEED** to know. One that, by knowing, will add a *massive* amount of value to their lives.

So to recap:

- → **Pick the topic**
- → **Brainstorm the title and subtitle**
- → **Book a call with me, and I'll take it from there**

HOW TO PICK THE ONE TOPIC THAT WILL CHANGE YOUR INDUSTRY

Personally, my suggestion is to pick a topic that:

- → **Most readers will benefit from hearing about**
- → **You are exceptionally well-versed in**
- → **You can write a book about**

The first two are important, but the last one is vital.

The easiest way to kill your book is to pick a topic that you would struggle to write 100-150 pages about.

To put this in perspective, pick a whale. Not a goldfish.

Imagine an ocean that's named after your industry…

Within this magnificent ocean is a variety of creatures…some big…and some small.

Your job is to find the creature that no one else would dare dominate. Something that is unique to you and your business. Something that no one else would ever try to talk about due to the overwhelming fear that they would accidentally be compared to you.

Every entrepreneur in the top 10% of their industry has a topic that they're exceptionally well-versed in.

What's yours?

If it's obvious, write it down and book a call.

If you need to think about it, my suggestion is to make a list. Then, prune the list using the three suggestions I listed above.

If you'd like, you can just write the list and book a call. Then, I'll help you weed out the bad ideas so you can feel confident in your book's topic before beginning your project.

Whatever floats your boat.

SUMMARY: THE THREE TACTICAL RULES OF THUMB

→ **Rule #1: The Reader Is Always Right**
→ **Rule #2: Presentation Matters**
→ **Rule #3: Judge A Book By Its Cover**

These are just three of the **INFINITE** (referring to my other book series) tactical rules of thumb you can use to craft a phenomenal **Authority Book**.

I got a few more bonus ideas to share before I get out of your hair…

Wait, that rhymed!

CHAPTER SUMMARY

☑ People love to say, "Don't judge a book by its cover." And I believe this is generally good advice with regard to most situations in life. Unfortunately, it's completely disregarded once people walk into a bookstore. Most people **have judged, do judge, and/or will judge a book by its cover.** Do with that information what you will.

☑ The easiest way to kill your book is to pick a topic that you would struggle to write 100-150 pages about.

☑ Just pick a topic that you believe your readers are dying to hear about. When I say dying, I mean…if this were the only book from your industry they'd ever want to read…this is the topic they would need to hear about.

☑ To put this in perspective, pick a whale. Not a goldfish. Imagine an ocean that's named after your industry…Within this magnificent ocean is a variety of creatures…some big…and some small. Your job is to find the creature that no one else would dare dominate. Something that is unique to you and your business. Something that no one else would ever try to talk about due to the overwhelming fear that they would accidentally be compared to you.

☑ Every entrepreneur in the top 10% of their industry has a topic that they're exceptionally well-versed in. **What's yours?**

THE ROADMAP

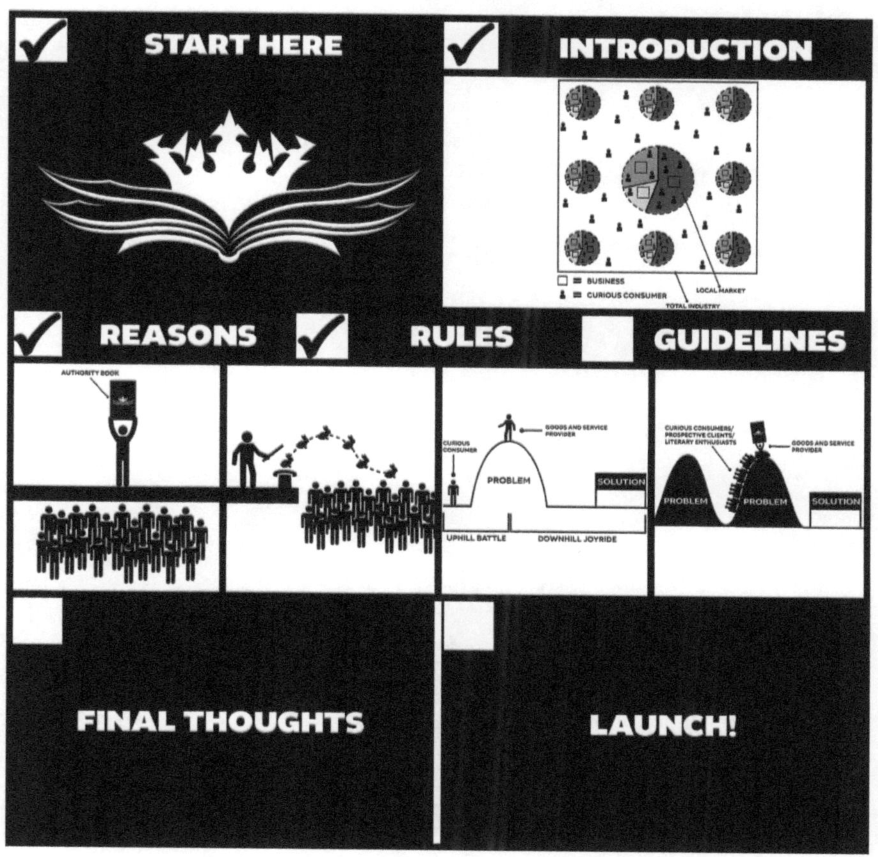

START HERE
INTRODUCTION
BUSINESS
CURIOUS CONSUMER
LOCAL MARKET
TOTAL INDUSTRY
REASONS
RULES
GUIDELINES
AUTHORITY BOOK
CURIOUS CONSUMER
GOODS AND SERVICE PROVIDER
PROBLEM
SOLUTION
UPHILL BATTLE
DOWNHILL JOYRIDE
CURIOUS CONSUMERS/ PROSPECTIVE CLIENTS/ LITERARY ENTHUSIASTS
GOODS AND SERVICE PROVIDER
PROBLEM
PROBLEM
SOLUTION
FINAL THOUGHTS
LAUNCH!

SECTION IV:

BONUS GUIDELINES
EASY AS 1-2-3

BONUS GUIDELINE #1:
TIMELINE

"If I had more time, I would have written a shorter letter."

— Blaise Pascal —

A GOOD AUTHORITY BOOK TAKES TIME

Good work takes time.

And I know you know this. I just need you to understand that it's true for this scenario as well.

I'm the publisher. So I cannot promise or guarantee any business results, outcomes, etc. that may or may not occur from you writing an **Authority Book.**

I mean, *technically* I could…but that would be unethical.

And by now you probably know…ineffective, inefficient, and unethical *isn't* my style.

However, I *can* guarantee one thing: **Authority Books,** if well-crafted, can help the top 10% of entrepreneurs, business owners, and experts dominate their entire industry.

Take the LTV (lifetime value) of a single client. Then multiply that number by the number of readers who, in the future, will want to work with you after reading your **Authority Book.**

An **Authority Book** is an asset. It's a tool to help you market, brand, and acquire clients at scale. The cost of creating an **Authority Book** is nothing compared to the cost of not having one. Especially if you are trying to expand past your local market and dominate your entire industry.

And if you don't believe me…this book is my business card, resume, proposal, magic trick…and *proof copy*… all in one.

Call it science. Call it art. Call it magic.

It works. And if it works for my business, it can probably work for yours too. With that said, I have two more **FREE BONUS GUIDELINES** for you to stuff in your pockets before you start writing *your* **Authority Book.**

But to reiterate this one: good work takes time. Proceed accordingly.

BONUS GUIDELINE #2: TRANSPARENCY

"A lie can travel halfway around the world while the truth is putting on its shoes."

— Mark Twain —

A GOOD AUTHORITY BOOK STREAMLINES TRANSPARENCY

Good work takes time, but bad work costs time, money, energy, and, in the absolute worst cases…reputation.

Said differently, **Authority Books** are a double-edged sword.

1. **Authority Books**, if well-crafted, allow you to extend the reach, intensify the impact, and amplify the communication of both your business brand and personal identity…
2. **Authority Books**, if well-crafted, allow curious consumers/prospective clients/literary enthusiasts to see beyond the veil of the corporate brand, enter your mind, and see the way your brain works…
3. **Authority Books**, if well-crafted, allow curious consumers/prospective clients/literary enthusiasts to enthusiastically calculate the probability of their problem being solved by you and your business…

Authority Books are designed to provide transparency, proof, and clarity as to **WHO** you, as the author, are.

If you possess the aptitude, integrity, and authority you claim to possess… the sky's the limit.

If not, then good luck!

Authority Books streamline transparency. Proceed accordingly.

BONUS GUIDELINE #3:
SET THE STANDARD

"We're not competitor obsessed, we're customer obsessed. We start with what the customer needs and we work backwards."

— *Jeff Bezos* —

A GOOD AUTHORITY BOOK IS THE BYPRODUCT OF YOUR STANDARDS

This idea is simple to understand, but hard to implement.

A good book is a collection of granular details, decisions, and choices all interwoven together to create a literary masterpiece for a particular reader.

When you write your **Authority Book**, you'll quickly realize…there are **INFINITE** different ways to say the same idea.

As a writer and, more importantly, as the authority of your industry, your job is to set the frame. The reader's perspective should be *set* by you. They should be viewing your industry through *your* lens. Otherwise, how can *they* see what *you* see?

You are the goods and services provider.
You are the guide.
You are the shepherd.
You are the authority.

Therefore, it's your job, as the writer, to set the standard so your prospective clients can understand what it's like to work with you *before* some of them actually *do* work with you.

Ruthlessly eliminate mediocrity.
Tolerate excellence and nothing less.
Showcase your personality.
Be the authority.

And let the rest take care of itself…

Your **Authority Book** is your business card, resume, proposal, magic trick…and *proof copy*… all in one.

Proceed accordingly.

THE ROADMAP

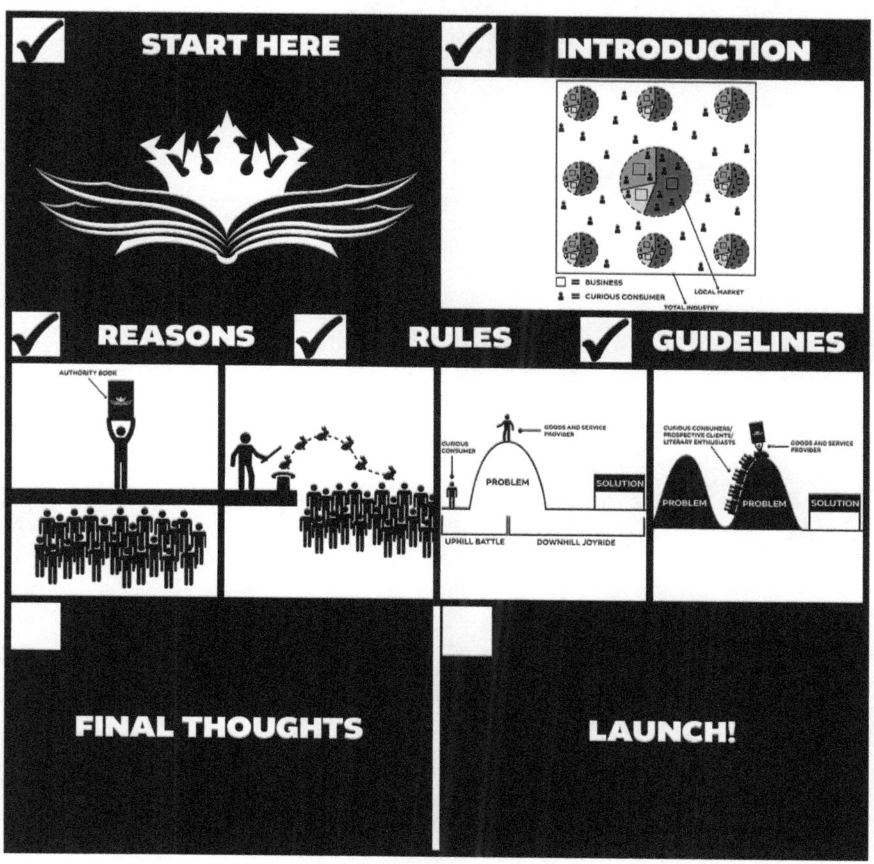

START HERE
INTRODUCTION
BUSINESS
CURIOUS CONSUMER
LOCAL MARKET
TOTAL INDUSTRY
REASONS
RULES
GUIDELINES
AUTHORITY BOOK
CURIOUS
CONSUMER
GOODS AND SERVICE
PROVIDER
PROBLEM
SOLUTION
UPHILL BATTLE
DOWNHILL JOYRIDE
CURIOUS CONSUMERS/
PROSPECTIVE CLIENTS/
LITERARY ENTHUSIASTS
GOODS AND SERVICE
PROVIDER
PROBLEM
PROBLEM
SOLUTION
FINAL THOUGHTS
LAUNCH!

SECTION V:

COUNTDOWN TO LAUNCH

FINAL THOUGHTS

> *"Every new beginning comes from some other beginning's end."*
>
> **— Seneca —**

Words, if used properly, allow us to make the vague and abstract clear. We deconstructed, operationalized, and explored a variety of complex concepts. Through reasoning, images, and strategic questioning, we were able to construct an integrated model of thinking that is tactical and timeless. **MISSION COMPLETE.**

It's been an honor.

And I look forward to making all of your writing, printing, and publishing dreams come true.

This book is subtitled ***"How To Dominate Your Entire Industry With One Well-Crafted Book."*** Whether you're an entrepreneur, business owner, investor, expert… or all of the above, the contents laid throughout the previous pages hopefully followed through on the aforementioned promise.

I love the beautiful game of entrepreneurship. Serve others, make money while doing so, and become a better person throughout the process.

It doesn't get much better than that.

With an **Authority Book**, you can play the game…at scale. Bigger, better, badder, and everything in between.

This book is my **Authority Book.**

Now it's time to launch yours...

Cheers to the future, let's work.

**Founder and CEO of Authority Book Launch
Founder and CEO of GPA Enterprises**

- Giovanni (Gino) Philipose -

THE ROADMAP

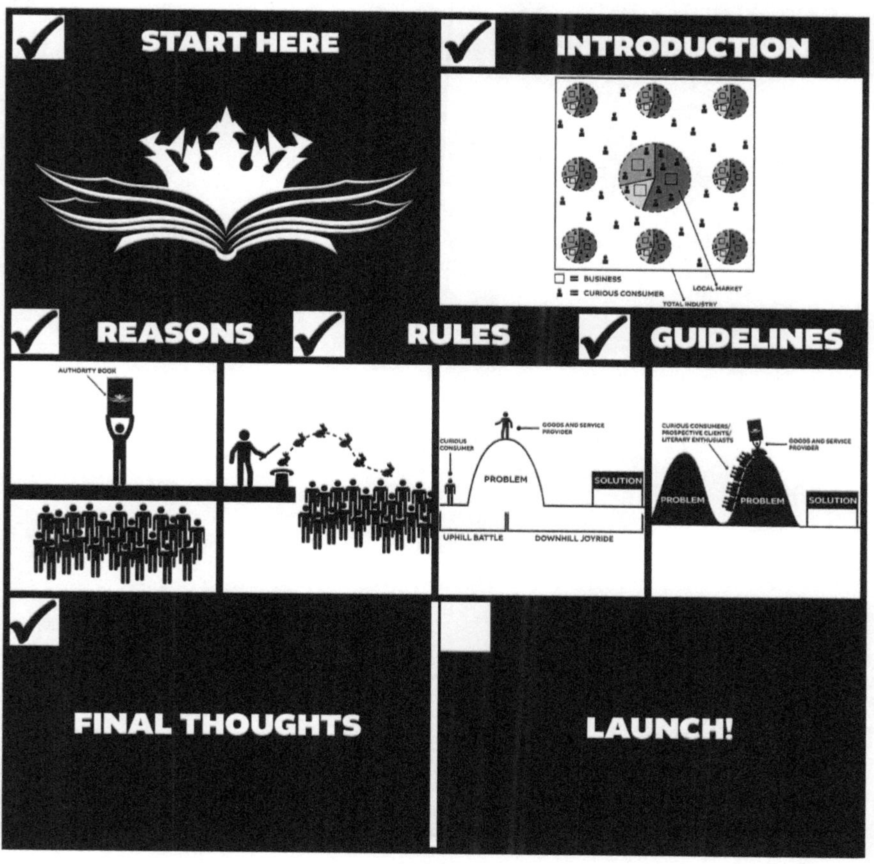

START HERE
INTRODUCTION
BUSINESS
CURIOUS CONSUMER
LOCAL MARKET
TOTAL INDUSTRY
REASONS
RULES
GUIDELINES
AUTHORITY BOOK
CURIOUS CONSUMER
GOODS AND SERVICE PROVIDER
PROBLEM
SOLUTION
UPHILL BATTLE
DOWNHILL JOYRIDE
CURIOUS CONSUMERS/ PROSPECTIVE CLIENTS/ LITERARY ENTHUSIASTS
GOODS AND SERVICE PROVIDER
PROBLEM
PROBLEM
SOLUTION
FINAL THOUGHTS
LAUNCH!

LAUNCH YOUR AUTHORITY BOOK

ALMOST TIME TO SAY GOODBYE...

Whew. That was fun.

The magic trick is almost over...

But, as the greats always say...

I have one last trick up my sleeve...

PREPARE TO LAUNCH!

This is the end of my **Authority Book**, but perhaps the beginning of yours...

So as you exit the literary auditorium with pockets overflowing with ideas, and prepare to re-enter the arena (AKA the marketplace), calculate your next move...*very* carefully.

There are authors.
Then there are authors with author-ity. (get the joke?)

We help entrepreneurs, business owners, and experts become the latter. Want to launch your **Authority Book?**

Here's how:

1. If you prefer to do things yourself, then take what you've learned here and go write your Authority Book. Then, when you have a 100-150 page message that you're ready to launch into the world, head to AUTHORITYBOOKLAUNCH.COM and secure the next available slot in our Core Publishing Program.

    →   **Then, once you've successfully followed the aforementioned steps, sit back…relax…and enthusiastically calculate the probability of us solving all of your *printing* & *publishing* problems…effectively, efficiently, and ethically…because we can take it from there!**

2. If you prefer a more streamlined & structured process, then head to AUTHORITYBOOKLAUNCH.COM and check out our menu of Guided Author & Publishing Programs to find the path that best suits your preferences.

    →   **Then, once you've successfully followed the aforementioned steps, sit back…relax…and enthusiastically calculate the probability of us solving all of your *writing, printing, and publishing* problems…effectively, efficiently, and ethically…because we can take it from there!**

3. If you're on the fence, then take as much time as you need to think on it. If you want to experience the magic trick another time, go reread your favorite parts of this book (if you had any). Sometimes you need to see the trick twice to catch all the details…

    →   **Then, if/when you're ready…**

Follow the road ahead…and good luck!

THIS MARKS THE END OF MY AUTHORITY BOOK

As I mentioned before, this book is my **Authority Book**. I figured, proof beats promise. This book in your hands is proof that what I offer…works.

My objective was simple: to show you my hand…and still close the deal. No poker face…no hidden agenda…no funny business.

Just…un-funny business?

Earlier, I guaranteed that by the end of this book, if you were amongst the top 10% of your industry, you would want an **Authority Book** for your business.

Then, once the demand was created…I would supply a certain percentage of the entrepreneurs who read this book with any and all resources needed to help their writing, printing, and publishing dreams come true.

Marketing, branding, and client acquisition 101. Right in front of your eyes.

Call it science. Call it art. Call it magic.

It works. And if it works for my business, it'll probably work for yours too.

Consider this book my business card, my resume, my proposal, and my magic trick…all in one.

Go back and study the details. Analyze the print quality. Step into my shoes. Imagine *your* words on paper in *your* prospective client's hands. Then multiply the number of prospective clients by 100. Then multiply that number by 100. And repeat this process until you understand the following sentence:

CONVERSATIONS. AT. SCALE.

That's what I offer. That's the power of one well-crafted book.

To conclude my **Authority Book**, I'll end with this:

There are authors.

Then there are authors with author-ity.

We help entrepreneurs, business owners, and experts become the latter.

Want to launch your Authority Book?

TURN THE PAGE TO INITIATE THE LAUNCH SEQUENCE

3

LEAVE A REVIEW

2

SUBSCRIBE & FOLLOW

YouTube: @giovanniphilipose
Instagram: @giovanniphilipose
TikTok: @giovanniphilipose
X: @gino_philipose
Facebook: @giovanniphilipose

1

SUBSCRIBE & FOLLOW

YouTube: @authoritybooklaunch
Instagram: @authoritybooklaunch
TikTok: @authoritybooklaunch
Facebook: @authoritybooklaunch

LAUNCH!

THE ROADMAP

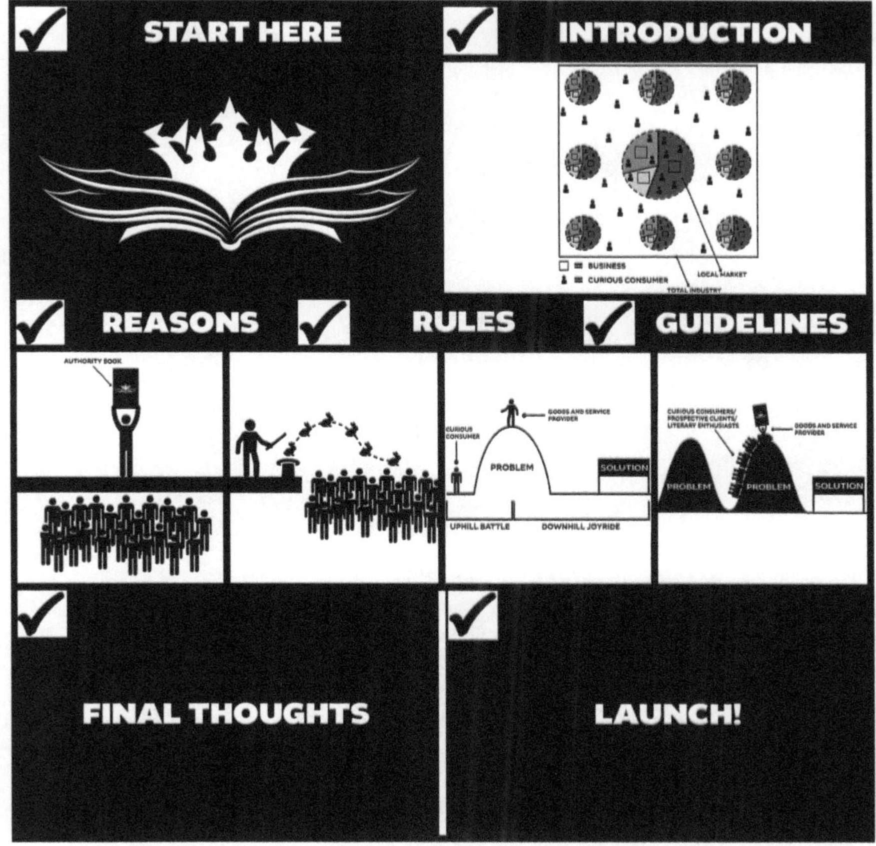

9 798999 552780